D1026504

"In *Days of Light and Darkness: Prayerful Reflections for Advent,* Sister Pamela Smith gives us all a precious Christmas gift: insightful thoughts about the season, delivered in small packages so we can't say we don't have time for God, faith, and prayer as we rush toward the holidays. Her own worthwhile daily meditations are augmented with mind-tickling invitations for reflection by readers intent on making the most of Christmas."

James Breig
Editor, *Evangelist*, newspaper of the Albany, NY Diocese
Author, *The Emotional Jesus: How to Feel Good About Feelings*

"Any book that helps us to take Advent seriously is welcome. Sr. Pamela Smith's reflections do just that. Scholarship, insight, and creative expression are woven together to offer believers a helpful hand in taking this glorious season into their daily lives. Particularly helpful are the questions and suggestions for further reflection."

Rev. Laurin J. Wenig
Author, *40 Days of Grace* and *In Joyful Expectation*

"Pamela Smith has written a forceful yet wonderfully poetic guide for the soul in *Days of Light and Darkness.* She has an insight into both the human heart and the heart of the Advent Scriptures which makes this book powerful! You should read it if you really want your life changed."

Bill Huebsch
Author, *A Spirituality of Wholeness: A New Look at Grace*

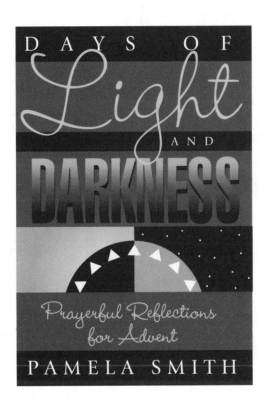

DAYS OF

Light

AND

DARKNESS

Prayerful Reflections for Advent

PAMELA SMITH

TWENTY-THIRD PUBLICATIONS
Mystic, CT 06355

in memoriam

Kenneth Vincent Smith

December 21, 1916 — March 13, 1962

a gentle man, a kind father

Twenty-Third Publications
185 Willow Street
P.O. Box 180
Mystic, CT 06355
(860) 536-2611
(800) 321-0411

ISBN: 0-89622-983-1
Library of Congress Catalog Card Number: 99-71176
Printed in the U.S.A.

Contents

Introduction

Shrubs domed with snow, spruce and pine branches lolling down under a white weight, a startling lightness of the landscape in the pitch of winter night: all of these are familiar northern sights as November's end leans into December, and Advent opens the way to Christmas.

The season's beauties can be taken as signs of what Advent means. The snow dome upon the shrubs suggests something of the Hebrew sense of glory, *kabod,* a coming down and covering over by God's own self, a heaviness which we welcome as it falls upon us.

The give and bend of the evergreen branches suggest grace and surrender, receptivity, and response. These are the very ways of being of the Christ, the man of self-emptying, the kenotic Christ. And they are the full expressions of discipleship, the welcoming of the wind of the Spirit and the weather of God's will.

The glisten of lake and field, city park and river bridge, the glow that awakens across forests and factory yards is the effect of gift, the allowing of light to reflect.

During all of Advent, our liturgies, our readings and hymns and candled wreath ceremonies, speak of the Light who has come, the Light whose glow persists from within, from the very much alive and very much today people of God.

We retell and remember salvation history with all its amazing hints and revelations, with its stumblings in the dark and ecstatic preparations for the Messiah, the Christ.

We recite the poetry and the bombast of the prophets.

We read our gospels retrospectively.

And we recall that the One who has come must ever come, anew and again, if our hearts, through the days and the nights and the changes of season, are to awake and awake and awake once more.

These Advent reflections, prompted by the cycle of daily Old Testament readings in the Roman Catholic lectionary and their gospel connections, arise from two age-old Christian convictions. The first is that the Christ, Emmanuel, God-with-us, has come once and for all and has irrevocably transformed our earthly human destiny. This faith-truth is the source of our hope. The second is that what God has done, God continues to do. And so Christ continues to prepare us to seek him, await him, discover him, and embrace him in our own time, in the salvation history that each of our life stories becomes. As we learn to see and focus, we open ourselves to Christ-sightings. He comes into our view.

From the shores of Orchard Lake, Michigan, from a seminary campus, and from more than a half century of my own journeyings and waiting, I invite others like me who love Christmas in all its depths and superfluities to revisit our faith story of love and splendor.

Amid the hurly-burly, we have to seize some moments of slowdown and *shalom,* some minutes of the day for Scripture and sanity. If we don't pause, chances are that we will miss the patience and poignancy which are the Christ story. And we chance forgetting the Light which still falls upon us new and lovely as a gentle night's snow.

Pamela Smith, SS.C.M.

FIRST
WEEK
of
ADVENT

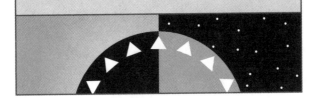

First Sunday of Advent

Year A   Isaiah 2:1–5 and Matthew 24:37–44
Year B   Isaiah 63:16–17, 19; 64:2–7 and Mark 13:33–37
Year C   Jeremiah 33:14–16 and Luke 21:25–28, 34–36

O house of Jacob, come, let us walk in the light of the Lord!
Isaiah 2:5

The readings from the prophets and the gospels for the beginning of Advent set us sliding back and forth on a well-oiled time track. We can look back with both nostalgia and pity, and then we can look ahead with cautious hope and yet no small apprehension. We look back six or seven or eight centuries before Christ and remember the Israelites who longed for swords to be beaten into plowshares, for mountains to quake and God's manifestation to vanquish every rebellious heart, for the house of Jacob to flourish, for a just "shoot" of Jesse to make all things secure and sound. At the turn of Christianity's third millennium, we can smugly settle back in our contemplative cushioned rocking chairs and satisfy ourselves that we are in the know. The One they vaguely hoped for has already come, some 2,000 years ago in fact, and we, of course, have happily been saved. We can parade out the pictures of christenings, first communions, confirmations, Catholic school graduations, weddings, and so on, as testimony to our churchiness.

But then the apocalyptic language of end-time looms before us in the gospels. There is still some mysterious appointed time, some coming of the Son of Man that promises to startle us and turn our lives topsy-turvy before the final global bang (or T. S. Eliot's imagined whimper), however it may occur. Tomorrow morning's news may announce that terrorists have blown up still more women and children in some far city or that the U.S. has launched a barrage of Tomahawk missiles against some oil-rich provocateur or, more locally, that some fury-driven child has gunned down classmates in a school cafeteria. Or we may walk blankly into some personal minefield: a shadow on a mammogram or the discovery of a PSA elevation, a middle management cutback that disbands our livelihood, the unexpected exit of spouse, friend, child, or love.

Heilsgeschichte, the ugly-sounding word that translates as "salvation history," has its glory days and its tragedies. The chosen people long and strive and falter and revive and anger and collapse and rally and then long some more for the Maker, the potter, the breach-mender, the champion to come on down and set them straight and pump them up again. *Heilsgeschichte* lives on. We Christians claim that salvation has happened, climaxed, that it can't be surpassed. But sometimes it sticks in our craw. Like the title character in Herman Melville's story "Bartleby the Scrivener," we're coaxed and cajoled to do *something,* to move or produce, and yet we continue with a blithe response: "I would prefer not to."

Our own salvation history is a long walk with cinders in our shoes and holes in our socks. In the background, Christmas carols jingle and sing-song, and we're safe as long as we don't pause to think about what it all means: Christ's coming, the call to discipleship, the invitation to live the Christ-life to the full, the challenge to supersede our mediocrities.

As we rehear the old prophetic cries and the Christian apocalypses, we need to enter Advent resolved not to spend our time being overly present to things past, or present to projected fantastic futures, but instead present *in* the present moment. Salvation and revelation *are.* The fulcrum of salvation history and eternal destiny is whatever we do here and now. We claim that the grand master of all our past and all our future is the One whom we call God-with-us, Emmanuel, the One who *is.*

If perhaps we were ever to grasp this, the todayness of salvation, the intimate presence-in-the-present of our God, it would trivialize our nostalgias and our comforts and also transform our businesses, our interpersonal crises, our blusterings and our anxieties. We would drop the prophetic and apocalyptic *will* and *shall,* let down our guard, and simply live the reality we sometimes read, sometimes sing, sometimes pray: "O Lord, you are our Father; we are the clay, and you are our potter..." (Is 64:8).

Then we would suddenly recognize that we can live in the house of Jacob, Leah, and Rachel and walk in the light of the Lord if we merely open a door, flip a switch. For the house and the light already are.

For further reflection:

Gerald O'Collins, in *Retrieving Fundamental Theology* (Paulist Press, 1993) has written: "Both in the documents of the Second Vatican Council and in important postconciliar statements, revelation is understood to have been a complete, definitive and unrepeatable self-communication of God through Jesus Christ. Almost in the same breath, however, this official church teaching also calls revelation a present reality which is repeatedly actualized here and now" (p. 89). O'Collins explains that when we speak of revelation we must also speak of salvation. In other words, "*saving* revelation" is what we both have and seek.

• How do I today experience the promise of the Messiah as "actualized here and now"? How, in my prayer and my day-to-day activities, does Christ appear as very present and new?

Monday of the First Week

Isaiah 2:1–5 and Matthew 8:5–11

*In days to come the mountain of the Lord's house shall be established
as the highest of the mountains, and shall be raised above the hills;
all the nations shall stream to it.*
Isaiah 2:2

Editor and translator John Stevens has commented, in *Mountain Tasting*
(Weatherhill, 1982), on the pressure and presence of mountains in the works
of the Zen poet Santoka:

> [M]ountains are the world of Buddha—vast, remote, sublime.
> Water and weeds are close to us, touchable, comprehensible;
> mountains appear mysterious, difficult to grasp…. Although
> mountains seem to be impenetrably high and wide, Santoka
> threw himself into their depth. "Westerners like to conquer
> mountains; Orientals like to contemplate them. As for me, I like
> to taste the mountains." (pp. 26–27)

In the Hebrew Bible, mountains are the sites of revelation and a symbol of yearning. The Great Theophany and the giving of the covenant with
Israel occur on Mt. Sinai. A great victory for the judge Deborah occurs at
Mt. Tabor. Elijah the prophet encounters God in a "tiny whispering sound,"
a "gentle breeze," on a mount we now call Carmel. Mt. Zion, Jerusalem, the
holy city, the home of kings and the temple seat, is the sign of God's fideli-
ty to Israel and Israel's longing to climb repeatedly to the exalted house of
God, to sing and praise and some day to dwell there lastingly.

Mountains impose their mystery and mystique on the religious imagination worldwide. Whether we hope, like the Israelites, to "stream to" the peaks
with a mighty multitude or whether we simply wish to gaze, assured in knowing that there is a God on high, the lofty mountaintops elicit awe and stir our

courage. They incite us to live upwards. As Santoka suggests, their height invites us to depth. Both height and depth invite us to experience.

Graying North American baby boomers know too well that one of the hazards of middle age is complacency. We can begin to feel that we've strained and climbed enough, gazed and sought enough, explored and tasted enough.

As many disciples also know—whether we are disciples of Jesus, of Talmudic scholars, of imams, of gurus, or of Zen masters—one of the hazards of any of our old-time religions is a kind of cozy familiarity that leaves us oblivious to new calls to growth. Like it or not, we need calamity and crisis if we are not to succumb to complacency and religious routine. We need startlement and detour if we are to come blinking upon new vistas. And we need our small worlds to drop out from under us if we are to be forced to raise our heads and look up.

The ancient Israelites, the faithful of the age of proto-Isaiah, had their split kingdoms, crazed kings, ceaseless military engagements, and waves of idolatry alternating with restoration. These opened them to messianic hope and the dream of a more glorious Zion, a godly Jerusalem, and an end to war.

Much later, in the time of Jesus, a Roman centurion had seen soldiering and triumph, slavery and bloodshed, authority and suffering. When he saw that his crisp command could not possibly conquer a servant's paralysis, he recognized his own powerlessness and his need for a greater, truly healing, power.

Like us, the people of Judah and the Roman centurion knew what it was for bravado to crumble. They knew that fortune could fail and that familiar paths dead end. At such times, they found that the only way to a life source was to seek one.

And so, like us, they learned that the only route to survival and sense was to look toward the mountains and to ascend to the realms of the All-Holy and the realms of healing. The only way to counter despair and meaninglessness was to look to the heights and enter the depths.

Amid cloud and smoke, if we are survivors and if we have living faith, we still can learn the way and touch the new. We can taste the green.

That is something of what Messiah-time, like Zen-time, means.

For further reflection:

St. John of the Cross, as is well known, chronicles the spiritual journey as *The Ascent of Mt. Carmel.* It is a journey that requires self-confrontation, asceticism, self-surrender, and darkness. It demands a turning and a turning again as we scale rocky heights and plumb treacherous ravines and rifts. While none of us who read this text may ever reach, or even aspire to, the heights of the sublime San Juan, we may perhaps identify with something of the arduousness of the journey, the darkness of dread and doubt.

• When I have experienced such stress or darkness, what has restored my vision and my confidence? What or who can I thank for angling my head up—to hope?

Tuesday of the First Week

Isaiah 11:1–10 and Luke 10:21–24

He shall not judge by what his eyes see, or decide by what his ears hear;
but with righteousness he shall judge the poor,
and decide with equity for the meek of the earth.
Isaiah 11:3–4

An artwork and a woman may be said to exemplify today's readings. The artwork is an American piece from the pre-Civil War period, Edward Hicks' *The Peaceable Kingdom*. Reflecting Quaker and Mennonite (and indeed authentic Christian) commitment to peacemaking, it displays a scene lush with life and creatures. The wolf and lamb, the leopard and kid, the calf and lion, the little child, the cow and bear, the infant and asp, the toddler and adder of Isaiah 11 all have their representatives here. *The Peaceable Kingdom* depicts the cessation of enmity and a gracious harmony of living beings with their own kind and with otherkind. Violence quells and provision is made for each to have its space and sustenance. Opposites are reconciled, and genuine righteousness and equity are held out in this optimistic view of earthly, godly possibility.

In Detroit, a woman who for more than thirty years has promoted harmony, solidarity, and possibility is Eleanor Josaitis. Along with Father Bill Cunningham (d. 1997), Josaitis made a commitment in the aftermath of the deadly Detroit riots of 1967 to erect, amid the ruins, some semblance of a peaceable kingdom. As white flight rampaged and unsold homes were boarded up, Josaitis, with husband and children, moved back from the suburbs to a besieged neighborhood. She and Cunningham piloted Focus:HOPE, a food distribution center and job training operation which today occupies six city blocks, educates technicians and engineers, feeds the disenfranchised, begins the schooling of neighborhood children with Montessori's best, and has multi-million dollar contracts with government agencies and auto corporations. The former Yellow Pages building has been bought out by Focus:HOPE and is in the process of becoming a hotel and restaurant management training center. Josaitis, now a grandmother, is the heart and the brains of Focus:HOPE, an agency with a mission to tap the talents, channel the energies, and empower the economically and culturally disadvantaged.

All of the Focus:HOPE work is done under a people-promoting, multiracial, mutually enhancing philosophy of the common good which rests on faith in the individual good. The nearby Church of the Madonna, which Josaitis attends, reflects the Focus:HOPE spirit. Black and white, Hispanic and Asian, Catholic and Protestant and the a-religious are offered abundant hospitality, a personal touch, vibrant liturgy, and a prolonged coffee and donuts gathering each weekend. During the week the church offers advocacy, home networking, and challenges to youth.

The artist of *The Peaceable Kingdom* painted into his work a conviction that there could be a time of easy coexistence and comfort among beings. The womanforce of Focus:HOPE built a multiplex human services and technological enterprise on the presumption that social change did not mean so much the making of truces between society's natural enemies as it meant awakening the commonalities of desires and dreams found in every human heart.

The readings from Isaiah and from Luke today speak of what the eyes see, what they may misapprehend, and what they may more clearly see if they look again. The Lord judges and acts, Isaiah says, not on first impressions, fleeting glances, or hearsay. Jesus reminds his disciples that infants may sometimes perceive accurately what is hidden from "the wise and the intelligent." He also invites his followers to look twice at him. He urges them to see that what prophets and kings have longed for is realized in him.

There is One, today's readings tell us, who overcomes evil, calms hostilities, reveals goodness and truth and beauty to those who see with fearlessness and clarity.

Today we are asked to question how fully our artworks, handicrafts, life projects and commitments are invested in him. How expressive and edifying of God's "peaceable kingdom" are our efforts and our very persons?

For further reflection:

The preface for the Feast of Christ the King in the Roman Sacramentary describes the "eternal and universal kingdom" over which Christ reigns. It is "a kingdom of truth and life, a kingdom of holiness and grace, a kingdom of justice, love, and peace."

• What portions of my life, and of my day, do I give over to these mainstays of Christ's kingdom? To what extent am I a representative and source of truth and life, holiness and grace, justice, love, and peace? And where do I compromise, fall short, back off?

Wednesday of the First Week

Isaiah 25:6–10 and Matthew 15:29–37

The Lord of hosts will make for all peoples a feast of rich foods,
a feast of well-aged wines…[H]e will swallow up death forever.
Isaiah 25:6–7

Messianic hope, in the age after the coming of the Messiah, is that the maimed have been healed, the tears wiped away, the banquet laid—or, at the very least, that the healing is in progress, the tears are beginning to dry, the banquet is in the making. Messianic hope is that goodness, richness, benefit are in the works and ongoing. Messianic hope is that God as giver of well-being and satisfaction is graciously acting. As Catherine Mowry LaCugna has explicated at length, the God of revelation, the God in Christ, is not only God-with-us but also wondrously *God for Us.*

Jesus declares to his disciples, "I have compassion for the crowd…" (Mt 15:32). And the act of his compassion is provision, providence. Messianic hope is the recognition that there is feast, that we, like the broken, hungry crowd of the gospel, are being filled. Faith is perhaps simply the clarifying of our vision: the locating of where and how we, amid our brokenness and hunger and longing, are indeed—and right now—filled.

We may, to our surprise, find that we are feasted and filled by a snow day that eases our schedule. Or feasted and filled by a kindness or gift. Or feasted and filled by the startling love and loyalty of a friend. With that, we recall that we are and can be daily feasted and filled by prayer, by word, by Eucharist.

Advent may invite us today to a sighting of the Messiah in life's extended liturgy. He is, here and now, in the Scripture we sit with, in the holy breaking of bread, and in the outflow and overflow of sacred space, symbol, and human love. Isaiah and Matthew remind us that God's gracious banquet-giving is in this world and of it.

For further reflection:

• For what do I say grace and give thanks this season, this day?

• Can I let a passage from the too early deceased LaCugna startle me into new life? She has written in her book *God for Us: The Trinity and Christian Life*:

> According to the doctrine of the Trinity, God lives as the mystery of love among persons. If we are created in the image of this God, and if our destiny is to live forever with this God and with God's beloved creatures, then what forms of life best enable us to live as Christ lived, to show forth the Spirit of God, and ultimately to be deified? (p. 378)

Thursday of the First Week

Isaiah 26:1–6 and Matthew 7:21, 24–27

The rains fell, the floods came, and the winds blew and beat on that house,
but it did not fall, because it had been founded on rock.
Matthew 7:25

In the Sermon on the Mount, the solid rock on which Jesus says we can found our lives is God's word and God's will. Isaiah, in his song of Judah, says that God, the one who is Lord forever, is "an everlasting rock" (Is 26:4), the one who truly deserves our trust.

Rock can suggest to us elegant cliffs to scale, boulders to lean on, smooth surfaces on which to sit, monuments on which we can engrave the legends of our lives and loves and national myths, Vermont fences, milestones, glacial deposits in Pennsylvania woods, sacred labyrinths, obelisks. There is beauty, in actuality and in possibility, in rock.

Yet rock can also be obstacle, stone wall, deadly slide or avalanche. Hard. Crushing. Insurmountable.

Is it possible that God is both?

It would seem that God is hard rock when we can't seem to hear or feel God's response to our questions and outcries. We can experience our prayer as echoes in a canyon banging back at us and fading, fading. God can seem to be encased in an impenetrable wall. When that is our experience, perhaps the call is to chisel God out. As Michelangelo knew that David and the Pietà lay, waiting and alive, within huge marble, we may find that only faith and trust can help us to see that living beauty can emerge as we hammer and cut away with our prayers, our cosmic doubts, our mutterings into night wind. Sometime, sometime, when the flash of insight comes (if we catch it!), we begin to see the art form of God within canyon wall, quarry, our personal stumbling blocks, the rough hewn slabs standing in our shops.

Then God can be safe and steady rock, too. Reliable, firm, holding the warmth of the midday sun. God can be the stone circle of our fireplaces.

There are moments, on a woodland path, when we can know that bark and deadwood, mulch, fallen leaves, moss, mud and frog, bird and pine needle, waterfall and red shale and granite, and, yes, our very selves, are all made of the same stuff—starstuff, Earthstuff, Godstuff. At such moments, rock softens for us, and we know with assurance that it does live and somehow slowly breathes.

When we think of the hardness and firmness of rock, we can think of the reliable God of Isaiah and Jesus, the God whose word and will and plan are solid foundation and steady shelter for us. But we can also recall that rock is of our world, within our art, locked into and linked in our lifechain, our web of life.

Rock makes a mighty rumbling when it falls and a slow slap when licked by waves. God's word and God's will are rumble and lull. What we need is to see, hear, understand, know.

For further reflection:

"Rock of Ages" is an old Christian hymn that somehow always conjures up images of Gibraltar. The fact that rock stands steady yet also wears and erodes with wind and water and time may invite us to a rich and paradoxical image of God as rock.

• How is the God of Jesus, our God, changeless yet changeable rock?

• What rocky scenes or stony places have been sacred to me?

• When have I worked with rock and discovered some hidden wonder?

Friday of the First Week

Isaiah 29:17–24 and Matthew 9:27–31

No longer shall Jacob be ashamed, no longer shall his face grow pale.
For when he sees his children, the work of my hands, in his midst,
they will sanctify my name; they will sanctify the Holy One of Jacob
and will stand in awe of the God of Israel.
Isaiah 29:22–23

Year after year, usually sometime around Easter, the Cecil B. DeMille extravaganza, "The Ten Commandments," airs on one of the networks. The God who calls forth Charlton Heston's Moses mobilizes a muscular yet wary man, tranforms him into a worker of marvels, fires him with *charismata*, and turns his hair white. God speaks, *basso profundo* and seismically, from burning bush and Sinai. He plagues and saves and sweeps waters into mountainous seawalls and drowns and leads. He promises and carves in rock. The God of Abraham, Isaac, and Jacob—the God of Sarah, Rebekah, Leah and Rachel, too—is a God of fearsome power and surpassing strength. To such a God the only appropriate response is awe.

Today's readings suggest, however, that there is another face to awe. Indeed, tyrants, scoffers, and exploiters do fall, Isaiah tells us. There can be exasperation and wrath in the one who awes us. But the awesome work of God can be gentle, steadying, healing too. Children live. The pallid, weary faces of worried parents regain the color of health and rest. The deaf hear, and the empty-handed and powerless come into their own in strength and joy. The blind see, as does the man in today's gospel who approaches Jesus not with trembling and dread but with simple confidence that Jesus can provide what he needs.

Any time we have been laid low and have then experienced some kind of comeback, we "stand in awe." It may be the sheer bliss of feeling how good it is to feel well. It may be the thrill of watching children dance and run and play with giggle and abandon. It may be the startlement of some beauty seen or pleasure met for the first time. It may be the amazement of being welcomed, sheltered, comforted, loved. We may be vindicated where we had been doubted, forgiven where we had been held off, reassured where we seemed to teeter. It may be the sudden realization that God has waited quietly and longingly for us in our gloom and shadows.

For us, then, God may at some moment be the God of Donder, Blitzen, Götterdämmerung—alarming enough to shake us awake, fearsome enough to redirect our ways. God can, and sometimes does, awe us into an absolute about-face. God can, and sometimes does, jarringly alter human destiny. And this provokes awe.

But it is perhaps more likely that at any moment God can awe us into gratitude. We can be, and are called to be, awed at what we hear, what we see, how we learn, what we know, how we pray, how we trust, what changes, what restarts, how life flourishes, whom and what we love.

For further reflection:

• The Shaker hymn "Simple Gifts" recalls things for which we can daily and over a lifetime be grateful. How often do I open myself to awe at simplicity, freedom, truthfulness, love?

• Hebrew and Christian prayer has a long tradition of "blessing" God for the good that God works, acknowledging the blessings that we have received, praising God for what is momentous for us and needed and timely. At what actions of God have I recently stood in awe? For what goodness, beneficence, do I stand in awe and bless God today?

Saturday of the First Week

Isaiah 30:19–21, 23–26 and Matthew 9:35—10:1, 6–8

Then Jesus went about all the cities and villages, teaching in their synagogues,
and proclaiming the good news of the kingdom,
and curing every disease and every sickness.
When he saw the crowds, he had compassion for them, because they were
harassed and helpless, like sheep without a shepherd.
Matthew 9:35–36

Winter wind stings faces, frost bites human ears and limbs, flu crushes chests with cough and wheeze. The crippled and the chronically ill fight for some sense of well-being day by day, in all seasons.

Isaiah knew that we may awake hungry and thirsty and be met with "the bread of adversity and the water of affliction" (Is 30:20) on leaden days. Jesus saw that sickness and helplessness surrounded him in every clamoring crowd. Yet both, the ancient prophet and the new rabbi, proclaimed good news. Isaiah proclaimed a God who hears and heeds misery, a God who sends a Teacher out from obscurity, a Teacher who points the way. God, declares Isaiah, is a giver of rain and greenery, a giver of light and a healer of wounds, a purging and justice-making God.

Jesus, himself the Teacher of righteousness par excellence, announces the nearness of the kingdom of heaven and gives health as its sign. He imparts to his disciples a power to heal.

Wonderful, yes? And full of promise!

But what about those of us who believe, pray, drink pure water, eat healthful food, revel in the light, thank God, and live with our braces and walkers, medications and shots, inhalers and pacemakers? The Christian who reads these passages about healing, restoration, and the kingdom of health can't help but wonder why it doesn't seem to be that way for him or her. Where is the good news amid the drudgery of managed care and major medical claims?

Those of us who have had, say, thirty years of disability or life-threatening illness to contend with can admit that there are days of anger and days of wary and even shaken faith. But there are also days of thankfulness and satisfaction. There are days of sun and days of radiant homefire. There are days of comfort amid cushions, warm baths, and loving arms.

There are days when we recall that, like the little girl to whom Jesus spoke "Talitha, kum," we do get up.

In Calvin Miller's *The Singer* (InterVarsity Press, 1975), there is a limp-limbed young girl who has been touched by the Singer, a Jesus figure. She does, in the story, rise from her twisted roadside position and run about in fields of flowers. But when she is asked what she wants to be when she grows up, she does not say a runner, a dancer, someone who skips, someone who walks without crutches. She simply responds with one telling word: "Alive."

For some of us Advent has brought the onset of an illness that lasts a lifetime. We have been helped by medical research and improved treatments. And even medical journals now verify that we have also been helped by churchgoing and a circle of prayer. We are alive, and we may be doing better than expected.

Total healing may not be ours, but fullness of life can be.

There is "bread of adversity" and "water of affliction" to this day. The Messiah has not made of our Earth a picture perfect paradise. We have not come to such beatitude. There is, however, healing touch and spring thaw. Of this, we can be sure.

God, godly people, and good friends love us into life. We are and can be, as we keep growing up and growing older, that one vital thing: alive.

For further reflection:

Relationships, touch, prayer, and self-care are holy and healthful activities, says minister Bruce Epperly in *Spirituality & Health, Health & Spirituality* (Twenty-Third Publications, 1997). A positive attitude toward our own embodiment and the bodily nature of beings is a way of reverencing creation and honoring God. Epperly observes, "Christian faith proclaims that the body is made by love and for love. In loving our bodies, we are loving the Creator whose love radiates through us. In nurturing the bodies of others, we are expressing God's love..." (p. 39).

• How do I love and praise God with my body? How do I celebrate the bodily being of others? How compliant am I with both the common-sensed and specifically medical prescriptions for my own care? How do I encourage others to take care of themselves and live holistically?

• Do I experience Jesus—in prayer, in sacrament, in others—as healer?

SECOND
WEEK
of
ADVENT

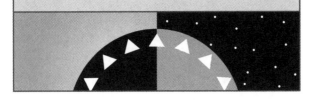

Second Sunday of Advent

Year A Isaiah 11:1–10 and Matthew 3:1–12
Year B Isaiah 40:1–5, 9–11 and Mark 1:1–8
Year C Baruch 5:1–9 and Luke 3:1–6

*Take off the garment of your sorrow and affliction, O Jerusalem,
and put on forever the beauty of the glory from God.*
Baruch 5:1

The reign of peace and the comfort of people, the gathering of nations into joy and light are themes of the age-old prophets—and promises that still stir our hearts. The voice crying in the wilderness, the voice of the camelhair-clad John, echoes across the ages promising spirit and fire. John tells of a great leveling and a salvation which "all flesh shall see" (Lk 3:6).

What Baruch calls the Jerusalem-to-be is "Righteous Peace, Godly Glory" (Bar 5:4). That is the city's name, the people's possibility.

Advent, in the end, it seems, is the messenger of our call to become what we already are, our mission to actualize our potentiality. The clothes of victory, the garb of splendor, the festal wear are sewn and already fitted for us. The widow's weeds, the torn uniforms, the camouflage suits, the raggedy hand-me-downs, the street-stained and dumpster-daubed bagman and baglady getups can be cast off.

The *if* is the key. People can live in peace, the poor can be cared for, the wounded can be healed, the hurting can be held and comforted *if* we worship God rather than the GNP, God rather than our creature comforts, God rather than our tax cuts, God rather than our toys and gadgets, God rather than our World Wide Webs and Internets, God rather than our excesses, God rather than the so much that we waste.

Christ has already come. Love in its fullness has taken human form. We have been told that a change of our minds, a quickening of our hearts, a turn in our walkways are all that is needful for us to love and for love to come for us.

25

Yet we are still waiting for love. We still wear our garments of affliction, our mourning clothes.

Do we perhaps think that after John the Baptizer, after Jesus, after the Spirit simmering in our own beings, someone else should still come?

The maddening thing about us is our refusal to notice love, our shunning of opportunities, our preference for dolefulness rather than light, our reluctance to be the glory and greatness and generosity we have received.

We are enough to drive still more prophets wild, drive them back into deserts to munch locusts and suck honey morosely and wonder what on Earth it takes to shake us awake.

Or who?

Again, who?

For further reflection:

• Who else?

Monday of the Second Week

Isaiah 35:1–10 and Luke 5:17–26

When he saw their faith, he said, "Friend, your sins are forgiven you…
[S]tand up and take your bed and go to your home."
Luke 5:20, 24

The ultimate freedom perhaps is assurance of forgiveness. Why? Because what forgiveness means, at heart, is that we are clearly perceived and deeply known and loved in our scars, weaknesses, misdeeds, and regrets. We are loved in our life stories, in their cripplings and paralyses, and told that we are not terminal, bedfast, sentenced to death but, instead, capable of walking on. We can pick up what we have lain down on and go home.

Going home seems a strong symbol of that ultimate freedom. For the follower of the Messiah, the ultimate homeland is heaven. And what heaven means is not some tropical spa or frothy cloudscape turned dance floor but the embrace of God. Going home means at-homeness with ourselves and with fullness of Being. Going home indeed means at-homeness with all beings.

Freedom and homecoming mean, it seems, the fruitfulness of forgiveness: making peace with frailty and fragility. Forgiveness does not mean settling for what is less than best or advocating some sort of anything-goes tolerance or laxity. What it does mean, though, is knowing that the sinfulness and selfishness that cripple us can be loved into ineffectuality. We can be straightened and strengthened.

What it takes for us to be able to walk freely and to go home is several things: our own awareness of our paralysis and crippling and the will to be well; the support of faithful and faith-filled friends; a direct approach to the divine physician. We have to be willing even to let ourselves be dropped through a roof for him.

What the Messiah meant for the paralytic he means, faith says, for us: a loving gaze, a healing touch, a confident command to get up and be our stronger, healthier selves. He assures us that his gentle strength is enough.

Isaiah's image of shalom is blossoming desert, healed people, a safe highway back to Zion: home.

Jesus the healer can give us, in its fullness, shalom. All we need is the freedom to seek and the readiness to receive even greater freedom.

Rising up from our beds of frustration and pain is what comes from Messiah-meeting. Which can come, we believe in these post-Resurrection times, every day.

For further reflection:

One of the notable things about us Christians is our lack of bashfulness about admitting that we sin. We have abundant assurance that God loves us in spite of everything and that forgiveness, imparted in Christ's death and resurrection, is lastingly and repeatedly given.

The danger to us, then, is not that we go unforgiven. It may be, rather, that we do not grow. We can easily become complacent in our sins and blithely resistant to genuine change. We can presume upon God's mercy and understanding.

The imagery in today's readings suggests, however, that forgiveness impels us to growth and change. The paralytic takes a new walk. The deserts blossom, and a healed people follow a new highway to Zion.

• In what areas of my life do I resist change while simply relying on God's compassion? Where may I be challenged to take a new walk? How can I overcome spiritual inertia and move toward growth?

Tuesday of the Second Week

Isaiah 40:1–11 and Matthew 18:12–14

A voice says, "Cry out!" and I said, "What shall I cry?"
All people are grass, their constancy is like the flower of the field.
The grass withers, the flower fades, when the breath of the Lord blows upon it;
surely the people are grass. The grass withers, the flower fades;
but the word of our God will stand forever.
Isaiah 40:6–8

Anyone who listens attentively to the readings of today might not be unduly surprised if, rather than a homily, an alto and soprano appeared in the sanctuary to sing the aria from Handel's "Messiah" which begins, "He shall feed his flock." The selection from Isaiah concludes, after all, with the image of the Lord carrying the sheep in his bosom, and the passage from Matthew tells us of the shepherd who leaves the flock of ninety-nine to rescue the wayward one. The image of God as gentle shepherd is familiar, well liked, comforting.

But there are other images, aside from that of cute, though not altogether reliable, sheep that appear to describe us today. We are prisoners or indentured servants whose God comes to announce that we have served our term; debtors whose fine is paid (Is 40:2). We are wilderness, desert, valley, mountain, rough road that God has to level and smooth (Is 40:3–4). And we are fields of grass sprinkled with wildflowers.

We are, thus, lush and unruly, lovely and inconstant. What prophet and poet invite us to is this God's-eye view of ourselves and our human world. Three adjectives among the so many possible describe us well: contingent, transitory, beautiful.

It doesn't take an ecologist to know that we all could not be, that our coming to be and our continuance in being depend on a cosmic array of circumstances. Collisions and comings together of molecules, matings, migrations, and weathers factor into our being born, developing, continuing in health, and prospering. Faith and our religious imaginations tell us that behind all these happy coincidences on which our lives are contingent is God's providential design.

The obituary pages of our newspapers remind us that we are transitory, as do news reports of sudden and tragic deaths. Changes of seasons, cycles of weather, migratory patterns of birds, the molt and fall of feathers and leaves, the crushed baby bird in the front yard, the roadkill along our interstates remind us that all is passing. We know by faith and human experience that change is the stuff of rebirth and renewal. We know that transitoriness gives our planet its vibrancy and implants in us a desire for lasting love and God. Our transitoriness is fearsome and beautiful.

That we are beautiful, even in our wildness and passion, even in our decrepitude and age, is the testimony of literature, music, art. The Pulitzer Prize winning novelist, poet, essayist, and short-story writer Alice Walker recounts how for many years she was ashamed of the damages to her eye caused by a childhood accident. She became bashful and hang-dog in her sense of ugliness. The day when her young daughter exclaimed in wonder that Mommy had a world in her eye was a transformative moment for Walker. What she had seen as a despicable scar, her daughter saw as something fascinating and lovely, an image of our blue planet. Faith tells us too that the God who loved creation into diversity, strangeness, and unexpectedness perceives us as beautiful in our aliveness and unpredictability—with our gracefulness and with our scars.

The message of the prophet and the message of the Messiah is that we remain unable to see the beauty in our contingency and our transitoriness until we rest in the steady arms of the loving God of Life. We remain lost, mistrustful of ourselves, others, and our world until we give over to the shepherd and begin to see from the vantage point of one who is carried and cradled, an errant sheep.

For further reflection:

• Shepherding is hardly a common occupation in our age of information, free trade, and high technology. How is it that images of Christ as good shepherd, the Twenty-third Psalm, and artistic and musical depictions of sheep and shepherd themes continue to be popular in our churches? When has the image of the good shepherd held the most appeal for me? How can I relate to the image of myself as sheep in need of feeding, tending, rescuing?

• Grasses and flowers are symbols of fruitfulness and bounty and often suggest restfulness and beauty to us. How can I see myself in Isaiah's image of grass which springs green and yet withers or in the image of the flower which bursts forth colorful and firm yet fades and wilts? Am I, in my spiritual life, an annual or a perennial?

Wednesday of the Second Week

Isaiah 40:25–31 and Matthew 11:28–30

Those who wait for the Lord shall renew their strength, they shall mount up with wings like eagles, they shall run and not be weary, they shall walk and not faint.
Isaiah 40:31

We need to soar. We need to exult and hope. Yet there are days—and there may be many of them—when we feel that whatever wings we might have are stunted, flaccid, hopelessly bent, misshapen. There are days when we feel that we can neither fly nor emit one note of what could be an ascendant song. We are overtaken with weakness, weariness, hopelessness, loss.

Faith, however, says that we need not remain in such a state. Not, that is, if we can come to recognize that we do not fly on our own mere strength. Not if we recognize that the wind does its work. We rise and glide not only if we will to lift our wings but also if we relax into being boosted and carried.

Soaring, exulting, hoping are a double work, half or less of which is ours. We want and raise our wings, whatever their shape. We foray forth and aloft, with whatever breeze and sky and impetus are provided.

Jesus promises an easy yoke, a light burden.

Isaiah promises an eagle's grace and God-given strength.

Orchard Lake promises swans, ducks, geese, crows, cardinals, a startling falcon, even as winter lingers. Even before days lengthen again.

And a night wind tousles the hair, flaps scarf and windbreaker, whisks old brown leaves across the walker's path even as it clears the way for another spring.

We wait, gradually raised.

For further reflection:

• What human and godly things do I rely on to renew my strength?

• When do I soar?

• In what, in whom, do I find hope?

Thursday of the Second Week

Isaiah 41:13–20 and Matthew 11:11–15

Now I will make of you a threshing sledge, sharp, new, and having teeth;
you shall thresh the mountains and crush them, and you shall make the hills like
chaff. You shall winnow them and the wind shall carry them away,
and the tempest shall scatter them.
Isaiah 41:15-16

Violence and upheaval can, we uneasily hear, surround the action of God.

Jesus in the gospel of the day speaks of the kingdom taken by force, borne away. God promises in Isaiah the power of threshing sledge and winds strong enough to carry off mountain dust. Both proclaim a God who breaks, shakes, pulverizes, sifts, incites, a cyclonic God whose kingdom suffers assault yet also does the shattering.

Jesus is no advocate of violence. Isaiah's image of threshing sledge is the implement that overcomes aridity and opens up rivers and fountains for the poor and the needy. But both see that change and the coming to be of God's reign stir violent resistance and require violent response.

In days past, a type of monastic and conventual asceticism encouraged "doing violence" to oneself. What the injunction implied was that only a severity of discipline, rigors of fasting, sensory deprivation, sometimes self-flagellation, could break flesh into submission and ready the spirit for union with God. Today such an approach has largely been abandoned, as psychology has shown how readily it smacks of masochism.

Yet we find that a kind of doing violence to ourselves is a requirement of mere Christianity. Training in nonviolence and conflict resolution requires that we do violence to our instinctive aggression. Simplifying our lifestyles and tithing on behalf of the poor or the environment require that we do violence to our tendencies to acquisitiveness and hedonism. Breaking patterns of addiction requires that we violently resist our insuperable drives and desires. And the history of the latter half of the twentieth century has shown that bringing down Soviet communism, British colonialism, American racism, a dictatorship in the Philippines in the Gandhian style of *ahimsa* and nonviolent resistance requires that we violently retrain and restrain our inclinations to attack on behalf of our own self-preservation.

The violence of threshing and winnowing is a violence which radically alters and makes good. The violence of the reign of God, as Jesus proclaims it, is a violence which alienates, gives rise to enmity, even as it calls us to neighborliness, loving kindness, mercy, solidarity. It tears down to reconstruct.

It invites us to the violent, rending work of disarming our hearts.

For further reflection:

In Handel's "Messiah" the first bass recitative begins with a verse from Haggai. At the point at which the Lord declares "I will shake all nations, and the desire of all nations shall come," the bass voice literally shakes. A rumbling is built into the music.

• When have I found that I, or many with me, have had to be shaken before God could come?

• Any one of us can have our lives rent by catastrophe, crime, unexpected confrontation, or the jarring failure of a sure thing. When have violent, rending events disarmed me...and worked, in the end, to good effect?

Friday of the Second Week

Isaiah 48:17–19 and Matthew 11:16–19

"I am the Lord your God, who teaches you for your own good,
who leads you in the way you should go. O that you had paid attention…!"
Isaiah 48:17-18

There is something about us that is never pleased. We are capable of arguing ourselves out of our best opportunities, declining sincere offers of friendship, denigrating our greatest gifts, talking ourselves down from aspirations and dreams. We're waiting, we insist, for better timing, the more perfect arrangement, the ideal relationship, the virtuoso feat, the surer thing.

We have a bad habit of looking a gift God in the mouth and deciding we'd rather trust a God more to our specifications.

There is nothing new about us.

Judaeans and Galileans labeled John the Baptizer an oddity and Jesus a man given to sleazy associations and excesses of food and drink. The onlookers, we now see, lacked discernment, though they were reminded that "wisdom is vindicated by her deeds" (Mt 11:19). They preferred to wait for some other Messiah with another style and a different theme song. They wanted their prophets more upscale and less discomfiting.

We don't always see, from our up-close perspective, how much we are like them. Yet we mirror the sassy, never satisfied childishness Jesus commented on.

We have our lists of qualifications for a decent kind of God. We want one who goes easy on us, who puts us in situations of minimal stress, who arranges relationships that run smoothly, who doesn't vex our consciences with the neediness of others or implicate us in society's crimes. We want a God who cures our ills, soothes our souls, makes sure that others affirm and admire us, secures our jobs, shores up our belongings, protects us on highways, steers us away from tough neighborhoods, shields us from violence and poverty, keeps others off our backs, makes us feel good as we sit by fireplaces sipping cappuccino.

We want religious leadership to exhibit a certain type of style. Preachers, presidents, teachers of the faith should be neither too posh nor too sloppy, neither too intellectual nor too folksy, neither too self-indulgent nor too abstemious. They should challenge us lightly but not probe deeply. They may ask for a slice of our abundance for a good cause or two, but they shouldn't tap our substance. They should offer a creative proposal now and then but not really disturb the status quo. Like the God we want, they should make us feel at ease with ourselves and enhance our serenity.

In the end, then, we are often like the people Jesus complained about who wanted a different mood, a different tune, a different message from the ones with which the Baptizer and he presented them. We are often like the chosen people of Isaiah's time who wanted "prosperity," "success," "offspring," and "descendants" in perpetuity (Is 48:18–19) but wanted no prescriptions or pains.

We want a God who is a soft touch and a religion that is a cakewalk.

The readings of the day remind us, unfortunately, that if these are what we want we are not choosing the pathway of the law, the prophets, and the Lord who fulfills them.

We aren't even paying attention.

For further reflection:

• In what areas of my life does God make me uncomfortable when I let myself listen?

• Where might God be challenging my presumptions about what religion and religious leadership should be?

• What dance or dirge do I need to hear? to join?

Saturday of the Second Week

Sirach 48:1–4, 9–11 and Matthew 17:10–13

Then Elijah arose, a prophet like fire, and his word burned like a torch.
Sirach 48:1

Elijah, the once and future prophet, testified to God, restored breath to a lifeless widow's son, overcame the bloodied prophets of Baal, was fed and succored by an angel, and met God not in whirlwind, earthquake, or fire but in "sheer silence," "gentle breeze," a "tiny, whispering sound" (cf. 1 Kgs 17–19). Because he was swept away and has been said for centuries not to have died, an empty cup and a place await him, readied and set, at every Seder.

Jesus, within moments of the Transfiguration and the manifestation of Moses and Elijah, acknowledged the has-come/will-come tension. He observes, "Elijah is indeed coming and will restore all things" (Mt 17:11), and yet "Elijah has already come, and they did not recognize him" (Mt 17:12). Wherever there is affront to God and good, wherever there is call to turn again to the source and center of the universe, Elijah's voice again resounds. Wherever there is faithlessness, Elijah's fire licks at our doorsills, threatens to lap up even our sodden wood.

Elijah taunts us with the inadequacy of our idols, the incapacity of our God-substitutes, the unresponsiveness of our latest Baal: "Cry aloud! Surely he is a god; either he is meditating, or he has wandered away, or he is on a journey, or perhaps he is asleep and must be awakened" (1 Kgs 18:27). And we are seared.

Jesus is the once and future Christ. He has come and is coming, Christian faith asserts. But he has also gone unrecognized. We all too easily white-out his white-hot glory, cover his word with white noise, tamp down the fire he can start up in our consciences and hearts with sedative white tablets or whatever is our white lightning of choice—vodka, gin, martini, or every variant thereon. We whitewash his word so that we can remain exactly as we are.

Yet Elijah still has a mission to "turn our hearts" (Sir 48:10). Jesus continues to call us to "listen!" (Mt 17:5), to repent.

We can recognize Elijah and the Christ when they come, when they have come, as they ever come, today and again, only if we keep tinder in our hearts.

For further reflection:

• In the age-old "Veni, Sancte Spiritus," we pray, "Enkindle in us the fire of your love." What kindling do I need to stoke that fire?

THIRD WEEK
of
ADVENT

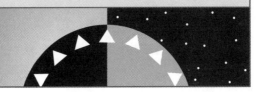

Third Sunday of Advent

Year A   Isaiah 35:1–6 and Matthew 11:2–11
Year B   Isaiah 61:1–2, 10–11 and John 1:6–8, 19–28
Year C   Zephaniah 3:14–18 and Luke 3:10–18

The Lord, your God, is in your midst, a warrior who gives victory;
he will rejoice over you with gladness, he will renew you in his love;
he will exult over you with loud singing, as on a day of festival.
Zephaniah 3:17

On Gaudete Sunday, the Sunday of pink vestments, a pink candle in the
Advent wreath, and an "almost" whispered in the hushed and waiting heart,
Zephaniah brings us the image of a singing Lord.

What kind of song could God possibly sing?

Matthew suggests that it is a freedom song—a song about what the
Messiah does for the blind, the lame, the leprous, the deaf, the poor; a song
about how God-with-us, the one in our midst, gives wholeness to the broken, meaning to those perceived as purposeless, life even to the dead
(Mt 11:4–5).

John suggests that it is a song of light (Jn 1:7), a song that we do not
know and cannot guess even while the song himself stands among us
(Jn 1:26–27), a mysterious song that comes after wild outcry in the
wilderness (Jn 1:23).

Luke suggests that the Messiah's song is a song of justice and generosity (Lk 3:11–14), a song of Spirit and fire (Lk 3:16).

Whatever God's song may be, it is a song of love and victory. We know
that there are times of prayer when a Taizé chant breaks from our being. We
know that there are times of ease when a whistle and a light step quicken us
down the street. We know that there are times of love when we hum a haunt-
ing, remembered melody and slide into a slow dance. God the champion,
God the festival maker, God the lover is there in every melody that awakens
in full hearts.

As Advent blossoms like Christmas cactus and we lilt from "O Come,

O Come, Emmanuel" into rounds of caroling, it is good that we listen carefully. In the well-known words, in the psalms of the season, but above all in the sighs and songs of our souls, we may hear, a prophet promises, God himself singing. He sings of all we need and long for, all we welcome and celebrate.

For further reflection:

• When irrational, inexplicable joy overtakes me, how do I sing out or express this joy?

• In the quiet and the dark, what song does God sing to me?

(Note: A shift to the special readings for December 17-23 may occur on any day from Monday through Friday of the Third Week of Advent, depending upon the date of the First Sunday in a given year. Reflections for December 17-23 are found in this text immediately following readings for the Fourth Sunday of Advent.)

Monday of the Third Week

Numbers 24:2–7, 15–17 and Matthew 21:23–27

"I see him, but not now; I behold him, but not near…"
Numbers 24:17

Jesus does not always, and maybe not even often, explain himself. Biblical scholars have long puzzled over and theorized about the "messianic secret," Jesus' instructions to his followers and even to demoniacs and demons not to reveal his identity. Christologists have pondered the extent and development of Jesus' own knowledge of himself, his identity, his mission. And in today's gospel we read of a time when Jesus declines to name the authority by which he teaches and speaks so familiarly of God. He turns the questions of the chief priests and the elders into another question—a question about whether John's baptism came "from heaven" or was "of human origin"—in other words, whether the Baptizer acted on divine impulse or merely on human inventiveness.

The religious imagination, if it is truly Christian, knows that God is both the revealed revealer and the ultimate unknown, that Christ is both the historical rabbi and the cosmic, creative infinitude. We know that the Holy Spirit is the stirring in our hearts, the fire in our church, the guide in our search for wisdom, and the ineffable, unpredictable, iconoclastic hoverer over churning waters and doorjambs.

This, of course, should not be surprising when we recall that we never quite fathom our own complexities. Nor can we navigate the rapids of our own psyches or map the minds and hearts of our best known and best loved friends.

45

As has often been observed of God's reign, God's kingdom, it is paradoxically "already, but not yet." The Messiah has come and is still coming. We belong to God and know our home yet remain strangers, sojourners, and at loose ends.

The oracle of Balaam, the oracle of one "who sees the vision of the Almighty" (Nm 24:16), tells of a star from Jacob, a scepter over Israel, a mighty one to come. And Balaam can only, in the end, use the language of paradox: "I see him, but not now; I behold him, but not near."

We see, but our vision is myopic; we hope and foresee, but we don't have present clarity.

There is always the more, always the mystery, always the aspect of being—whether God's or our own—which is not capable of being described or disclosed. Not now, anyway. Not in space, time, or human imagery. There remains that of which we can speak only in gasps and stutters. And yet, strangely, we do see, just as we see stars whose surfaces we can never hope to sift through our hands or adequately understand.

For further reflection:

• All of us perhaps have our favorite picture or sensory image of God. When do I realize, with a start, that my reassuring image isn't enough, maybe isn't even remotely on target? Have I ever discovered a "graven image" of God carved in my heart?

Tuesday of the Third Week

Zephaniah 3:1–2, 9–13 and Matthew 21:28–32

For I will leave in the midst of you a people humble and lowly.
They shall seek refuge in the name of the Lord—the remnant of Israel;
they shall do no wrong and utter no lies, nor shall a deceitful tongue be found
in their mouths. Then they will pasture and lie down,
and no one shall make them afraid.
Zephaniah 3:12–13

Amid a world of schmooze, spin, image-makers and p.r., we need sometimes to attend to the truth of a wild goose pecking where stiff reeds poke through a crackly coat of ice. We need the truth too of the men and women in shabby coats who revere soup and bread as feast. We need uncluttered scenes, honest answers, genuine gratitude in prayer.

As we listen to our teens and young collegians, we realize with a bit of a shock how much conscience formation and shaping of aspiration have been done, not by our catechesis and preaching, but by our malls, soundbites, top forty, videos, stadiums, ticketrons, credit card offers, night spots, climate control, spring breaks, top-of-the-line clothes, fitness centers, drive-up windows. We are surrounded and shaped by a culture of comfort, glitz, gratification, and quick fix. We are rewarded for our discontents and our unrequitedness and urged to seek, borrow, buy, acquire, upgrade, downplay, soothe, swallow, luxuriate, and then awake to the more that further stirs our yearnings. We demand that our news teams report if telephones are down or playoffs are postponed, but we channel surf if we happen onto a segment about starvation in Sudan or swastikas splayed on the doors of the nearby synagogue. We want our people movers high, fine, and streamlined so that we don't have to meet any unsavory sorts on the beneath-us streets.

If we feel a moment of unease, we make sure we allot a bit to United Way.

None of us middle Americans, I suspect, classifies ourselves among the oppressors, the faithless, the haughty blasted by Zephaniah or Jesus.

Yet we are hardly the remnant, the *anawim,* who are guileless yet timorous, underdogged and hungry, disadvantaged yet faithful, bereft yet hope-filled, unsure but singing "Soon and soon and very, very soon." We are not a remnant who know want or notice that we should. We are not the watchers, the waiters, the holy ones. And we are not laid-back, lolligag, easily led sheep.

We don't want to think that we are the "you" whom Jesus addresses when he mentions that lowlifes are "going ahead" of some folks into the kingdom of God. Though, of course, we're not tax collectors, prostitutes, or generic degenerates, either.

The question of the day is, under our cosmetics and coiffures, our aftershaves and musks, our cufflinks and gold chains, our makeovers and make-up, who are we?

For further reflection:

• As every reader of news magazines knows, the preoccupation of the notorious Jesus Seminars is the question of who the historical Jesus is, how we can relocate something of the "real" Jesus under the accretions of biblical composition and conversionist agendas. Maybe who *he* is is not the critical question, however. Maybe the question for people of faith is more properly this: how do we become real enough to meet him or know him when we do?

Wednesday of the Third Week

Isaiah 45:6–8, 18, 21–25 and Luke 7:18–23

"I am the Lord, and there is no other. I form light and create darkness,
I make weal and create woe; I the Lord do all these things."
Isaiah 45:7

There are days when throbbing blue-gray clouds turn charcoal. Lightning strikes. Streets are swamped. Roofs collapse under weight of wind and water. Any illusion of nature's perpetual benevolence is smashed as fires rage, flood waters pummel, carcasses collect.

Cheerful, backslapping Christians, chortling, sweet-talking true believers—the sorts who make ushers, greeters, hospitality committees, and amen corners—are hard-put to tell what this line about weal and woe might mean. Weal, that marvelous multiplex well-being and inner, if not outer, wealth, is what we chortle and backslap about. Grandkids, a cottage up north, a good buy on lawn chairs, a concert, a tax break, the right kind of cholesterol, genteel company on a Friday night, a quiet neighborhood assure us that life is good. Then again, for some of us maybe much less is enough. No one among family and friends is drunk, in jail, under a restraining order, being tailed. So all's well. God works.

The first reading and the second seem, meanwhile, to contradict. Christ makes whole, and God creates woe?

The readings invite us to think again.

All relationship and all response is, in the end, Godward. The world is filled with forces beyond our fathoming and control. While there is much that we can direct and choose, there are calamities that wrack us. It does not seem, in the end, that catastrophic illnesses or disastrous events have been planned against us. They do not seem personally designed to daunt or test us. That, at least, seems to be the conclusion of Old and New Testaments. The same passage in Isaiah which speaks of God as "creator" of woe also declares of God's Earth: "he did not create it a chaos" (Is 45:18). In other words, God does not and has not done deeds of malevolence, has not deliberately wrought havoc, is not engaged in a sadistic puppetry that stretches taut our endurance.

The testimony to Jesus, the testimony he himself points to in response to the twice-posed question, "Are you he who is to come, or are we to wait for another?" (Lk 7:19–20), is a testimony to his work on behalf of wholeness, his wresting weal from woe. The blind, the lame, the poor, the leprous, the shunned, the sorrowful are restored and held in hope.

It is perhaps too simple, too overworn, but the answer to theodicy's question seems to be an affirmation of God's goodness, God's benevolence, God's lordship over all creation. The catch is that God as creator has created a world of freedom, a world in which, as Thomas Aquinas asserts, chance can also be operative in an ultimate providential plan. Where there is freedom and chance, there is the possibility that some beings, ourselves included, may be harmed. But both Isaiah and Jesus proclaim that if we turn and turn again when we have withstood harm or when we seem overwhelmed with woe, there is still a curative and conquering weal which can come.

We find strength to withstand disability or disaster and find that new creation, rather than crushing chaos, can come of it.

That seems, in the end, to be how we experience omnipotence: God's power for us, with us, infused into us, is a power that makes well, makes good, shapes new worlds where we thought we knew ruins.

For further reflection:

Gretel Ehrlich, in *The Solace of Open Spaces* (Penguin Books, 1985), writes of the healing effects, amid the tragic loss of a deathbound love, of Wyoming's stark, almost arctic winters, its floods and deserts, its wide loneliness, and hard laboring, laconic people. She attests that she found new strength, new life, a new reason for writing, and new love in a land of Native American sun dances, cowboys, sheepherders, and lightning strikes. She does not name the source of such healing the "messiah" or "Christ." Instead, she speaks of help, nurturance, camaraderie, community, endurance, resignation, the will to overcome and live on which she witnessed in Wyoming's wild landscape.

• How might I argue that such an experience—and my own personal experiences of restoration and comeback—are assuredly the work of God as well as benefits of nature and humanity? Does it matter whether I/we know the God-in-it or not?

Thursday of the Third Week

Isaiah 54:1–10 and Luke 7:24–30

Sing, O barren one who did not bear;
burst into song and shout, you who have not been in labor!
For the children of the desolate woman will be more than the children
of her that is married, says the Lord.
Isaiah 54:1

All of us, sad to say, have met singles who felt they were alone not by vocation, but by default. We have also encountered childless couples who longed for children yet have been able neither to conceive nor adopt. We have known of miscarriages and crib deaths. We have heard the heartbreak of a spouse deserted at midlife, stunned to learn that a long-term partner had been romancing someone else for a considerable while.

In the opening verses of Isaiah 54, the Maker of Israel is shown to be a source of "great compassion" and "steadfast love," a devotion that one can count on. Even when we feel bereft and barren or, whatever our marital status or gender, somewhat "like a wife forsaken and grieved in spirit, like the wife of a man's youth when she is cast off" (Is 54:6), Isaiah asserts that divine love can be trusted to support us everlastingly. Though we may feel used and used up, empty and purposeless, God promises that oases can burst and blossom from our desert.

Three figures, at least, appear in today's readings as recipients of that promise: Elizabeth, John the Baptizer, and us.

Elizabeth is one such recipient of God's "great compassion." Indeed, Zechariah's canticle hails the arrival of their late-life child as a result of God's mercy, God's tenderness. Our scriptural knowledge of Elizabeth is scant. We know that she couldn't conceive and then finally did when she was "getting on in years" (Lk 1:7). We know of her familial bond and spiritual relationship with Mary. The two seem representative of women marked for blessing in Isaiah 54:1—a barren woman and an unmarried one, both of them roused

51

to "song and shout" by the uncanny ways of God. Elizabeth stands in the background of today's reading from Luke. Jesus declares that "among those born of women, no one is greater than" her son John (Lk 7:28). A woman whose life for years must have been weighed down with disappointment and drudgery finds herself an agent of the messianic age, a progenitor of a change in history.

John the Baptizer, also childless, appealing to the disreputable, rebuked by the esteemed (Lk 7:29–30), knowing he would be and should be overshadowed by Jesus (Lk 3:16), yet not always sure where his gathering of disciples ended and Jesus' began, may well have wondered what his life and mission meant. His role in the salvific scheme of things seemed not entirely clear as wilderness solitude led into rivers of baptism, and words of admonition led to a summons from Herod's axman.

But in the lives of Elizabeth and John, meaning amid mystery, purpose amid puzzlement, are the final resolve. She plays her role, he his in the unfolding of a saving plan. In spite of life's long thirst, God's promise is fulfilled. No more "waters of Noah" would swamp the parched, and God vows, "my steadfast love shall not depart from you" (Is 54:9, 10).

So we too may hope. We have God's word of love. We have the greatness of the kingdom. We live a story larger than ourselves and have a part in what even scoffers call the "Jesus movement" that moves into its third millennium.

Scripture assures us that seeming is not the sum of our meaning.

For further reflection:

A segment of this reading from Isaiah, with a slight shift in verses (Is 54:5–14), appears not only on this Advent day but also as the fourth reading in the Old Testament series proclaimed before the *Gloria* at the Easter Vigil.

• How does the theme of everlasting love and unshakeable peace come through for me in our preparations for both Christmas and Easter?

• How has God's love for the "forsaken and grieved" touched my life personally?

Friday of the Third Week

Isaiah 56:1–3, 6–8 and John 5:33–36

And the foreigners who join themselves to the Lord, to minister to him, to love the name of the Lord, and to be his servants,…these I will bring to my holy mountain, and make them joyful in my house of prayer.
Isaiah 56:6–7

There are remarkable and grace-filled people who have a facility for extending hospitality and warmth to everyone. They exude welcome. Family, friends, guests, and strangers feel relaxed and refreshingly at home in their presence.

The dwelling place of God is shown, in the reading from Isaiah, to be like haven and home for foreigners and outcasts. God is a sheltering God who lovingly invites love, loyalty, ministry. God responds to those who do love, do remain loyal, do minister in his name.

John the Baptizer was one such person. He was, as Jesus attests, "a burning and shining lamp." Those who responded to his service of prophecy, preparation, invitation to repentance "were willing to rejoice for a while in his light" (Jn 5:35).

John, like anyone we call saint, drew people because he bore something of God's dwelling into the midst of everydayness on Earth. He realized and radiated something of the warmth and light of God's "holy mountain." Even its ferocity, even its compelling lure.

He exuded the hospitality, the haven, the ever-lit lamp of prayer.

We who have been drawn, even long ago, by hope and love and light may ask ourselves if we yet stand as "burning and shining lamp," as a kind of lighthouse for our compeers and our culture's many seekers. If not, we need to examine ourselves about where our joy has gone, what has dimmed us.

For further reflection:

• How might I share the story of the way Godlight has drawn me and kept me on course?

• How might I extend myself more fully to the "foreigners" and "outcasts" around me and offer my small light?

(Note: This is the last date on which readings for the Third Week of Advent are used. If the shift has not already taken place, hereafter the readings for December 17-23 are used. As noted above, they are found in this text after the readings for the Fourth Sunday of Advent.)

Fourth Sunday of Advent

Year A Isaiah 7:10–14 and Matthew 1:18–24
Year B 2 Samuel 7:1–5, 8–11, 16 and Luke 1:26–38
Year C Micah 5:1–4 and Luke 1:39–45

"Joseph, son of David, do not be afraid to take Mary as your wife,
for the child conceived in her is from the Holy Spirit."
Matthew 1:20

In the liturgical calendar of the Chaldean rite of the Catholic Church, the Fourth Sunday of Advent is celebrated as the feast of St. Joseph. He is riddled through today's readings, whatever the year, in the Latin rite. The passage from Isaiah assures Ahaz of the staying power of the "house of David," foretells a remarkable pregnancy, and announces its result, the birth of Emmanuel (Is 7:13–14). Some three centuries before the prediction to Ahaz, David, desirous of building a temple but held back, had received the pledge: "Your house and your kingdom shall be made sure forever before me; your throne shall be established forever" (2 Sm 7:16). Micah too foretells the coming of a ruler, one "whose origin is from of old, from ancient days" in Bethlehem of Ephrathah, David's home (Mi 5:2).

Joseph and Mary are the inheritors of the promise—Joseph, traced genealogically to David (Mt 1:6, 16; Lk 1:26; 2:4; 3:23, 31); Mary, angelically and Spirit-bonded to the house of David by mothering the one called "Son of the Most High," the one destined to occupy "the throne of his ancestor David" (Lk 1:32). Of course, the link of Joseph and Mary with royal heritage and messianic destiny has its ironies.

Joseph is a carpenter, rough-hewn, silent. He acts: takes Mary as his wife, travels to Bethlehem, flees by night to Egypt. No words of his are ever recorded. Joseph dreams and listens.

Though Mary is recorded as having tucked away many things into a quiet, contemplative heart, she gives voice to questions and expressions of faith, most sublimely in her Magnificat (Lk 1:46–55). Her prayer, in its own way, shows an awareness of God's own irony. If indeed the house of David is to be fulfilled and his throne secured for all time by the coming of her boychild, this is a subversive event, an inversion of the social order, an upheaval of power relations: "He has brought down the powerful from their thrones, and lifted up the lowly; he has filled the hungry with good things, and sent the rich away empty" (Lk 1:52–53). She is an unknown from Nazareth. According to Luke Timothy Johnson in *The Real Jesus,* the Talmudic passage Sanhedrin 106a associates her with a "sex scandal," presumably because of the dubious circumstances of Jesus' birth. The reputed father, Joseph, has less said about him in all of Scripture than is said about David's father, Jesse. Jesse, by the way, also speaks, commanding David to take food to the encampment against the Philistines (1 Sm 17:17). Both Joseph and Mary have less written about them in Scripture than is told of Ruth, the great-grandmother of David.

It is as if to say that doing and dreaming, being reverent and attentive, waiting, pliable and ready, suffice. The royalty of Joseph and Mary is in their undeterred courage and their elegant responsiveness. Mary says, "Here am I, the servant of the Lord; let it be with me according to your word" (Lk 1:38). And Joseph, when he "awoke from sleep, he did as the angel of the Lord commanded him" (Mt 1:24).

Joseph and Mary heard the word and did God's word in surrender and unknowing. The disenfranchised and dethroned are enthroned as a new realm of God comes to be. And Emmanuel is. That seems occasion for a saintly feast.

For further reflection:

Obedience, it seems, can change history and give great meaning to obscurity. St. Ignatius Loyola, in his famous "Suscipe" ("Take, Lord, receive"), exemplifies the way in which a slight man can generate a great movement, effective to this day in the Society of Jesus, by opening himself to God and laying his liberty, memory, understanding, and will at the service of divinity.

• What must I let go of so that I can, today, tomorrow, the next day, make myself more available, more surrendering, more ready to act—even perhaps silently—on behalf of God and the good?

FOURTH
WEEK
of
ADVENT

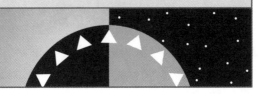

December 17

Genesis 49:2, 8–10 and Matthew 1:1–17

...[A]nd Jacob [was] the father of Judah and his brothers,
and Judah the father of Perez and Zerah by Tamar...and Boaz the father of Obed
by Ruth, and Obed the father of Jesse, and Jesse the father of king David.
And David was the father of Solomon by the wife of Uriah...and Jacob the
father of Joseph the husband of Mary, of whom Jesus was born, who is called the
Messiah.
Matthew 1:2–3, 5–6, 16

The genealogy of Jesus offered in Matthew seems, in many ways, a long line of missing mothers, of *incognitae* who bear children and disappear.

Noteworthy in this extended list of male ancestors from Abraham to David to Jechoniah and the return from Babylon and then to Jesus are the four women who are mentioned. Tamar, widowed, disguised herself as a roadside whore and bore twins by her paying father-in-law. Ruth was the Moabite widow whose loyalty to her mother-in-law led her to a new land and a new religion. Widowhood and female friendship prepared the way for Jesse and David. Bathsheba, the wife of Uriah, was the beauty who played a role, perhaps quite unwilling, in the adultery and murder for which David was held culpable. Mary of Nazareth was like the other three in that she would have remained otherwise unknown if she had not assumed such a stunning and altogether unexpected part in the lineage of salvation history.

A desperate woman driven to make something memorable of her life by bearing a child in her dead husband's name, a foreigner who gleans barley and wheat, a woman bathing who unsuspectingly allures a king gazing from his rooftop, a virgin promised to a carpenter who knows she has not slept with him: these are the female ancestors of Jesus whom Matthew deigns to note from the family tree. The unmentioned ones include worn old women and bright young ones, women of overwhelming loveliness and women scorned, pious women and mediocrities. With our prayerful surrender and yet also in spite of us, with our kindly deeds and amid our unthinking errors, Matthew seems to say, our God continues to work.

God wakes the world in the unlikeliest ways, through the unlikeliest of lives.

We end up touched, graced, and once again surprised.

For further reflection:

• As I scan my recollections of Genesis, 1 and 2 Samuel, 1 and 2 Kings, 1 and 2 Chronicles, can I identify the ancestor of Jesus with whom I can at least somewhat relate? Who? How and why?

• In the development of my own faith life, what role have mother, grandmother, great-grandmother, or other female relatives played? What women today help shape and support my faith?

December 18

Jeremiah 23:5–8 and Matthew 1:18–24

The days are surely coming…when I will raise up…a righteous Branch…
Jeremiah 23:5

On summer days, branches of hardwoods burst into light green, emerald, olive, the occasional dried mahogany. Birch, oak, maple, ash, poplar shine in dew and morning light. Slim new branches flex as passersby brush them on pathways. Old bent branches jut from mighty trunks and seem, at times, to hold up sky.

The one prophesied by Jeremiah, the "righteous Branch" raised up for David, is like one of those sturdy, sure branches which can give but not snap in windstorm, carry the weight of frozen water after icestorm and not crack, support shoots and offshoots and offshoots again from which spring's blossoms and summer's leaves unfold. Rooted deep, steadied in good soil, watered with generous rain, a "righteous Branch" can be fruit-bearing, letting small apples green into sweet autumn red.

Trees of life, the Jesse tree, vines and branches recurrently image Christian faith and the faith of Israel. Such faith trusts God as the giver and restorer of good land. It expects of God "justice and righteousness" (Jer 23:5) even where these have, for a time, been denied, abrogated.

Salvation, in the prophetic sense, seems to hold a this-worldly character as well as a promise of something later, beyond. The ultimate triumph of truth, justice, righteousness, simple good is, of course, a godly promise. But so too is the assurance that God's world ought to be a place of safety, freedom, good land, fair deeds. As we have come to realize through our twentieth-century terrors and our theologies of liberation, "salvation" is empty preaching if it does not act in some way for the provenance of good leadership, just systems, protection against violence and threat, means and access to learning and land.

Jeremiahs and Josephs, Rigoberta Menchus and Joan Chittisters know that God's justice must touch our lands, our relationships, our work and our lives. We must seek to live rightly, to decide righteously (Mt 1:19), to proceed along godly lines if our world is ever to go sturdy and green.

For further reflection:

It is well known that a worldwide synod of Catholic bishops in 1971 spoke of work on behalf of justice as a "constitutive dimension of the preaching of the gospel."

• How, in my life, do I express and embody that gospel commitment to justice?

December 19

Judges 13:2–7, 24–25 and Luke 1:5–25

Then the woman came and told her husband, "A man of God came to me, and his appearance was like that of an angel of God, most awe-inspiring; I did not ask him where he came from, and he did not tell me his name..."
Judges 13:6

"Angels watchin' over me" has its versions in gospel song and Christian rock, African Methodist Episcopal soul and whiter-than-white Baptist hymnody. Catholics sing "Dear Angel" prayers to their individual guardians, and a music minister, in a bemused moment, lilts his keyboard into "Somewhere Out There" as offertory gifts are brought forward on the September 29 feast of archangels. Angels show up as the wearisomely cheerful Clarence in *It's a Wonderful Life.* Michael Landon and John Travolta have played angels, as have hearty Della Reese and pert, chirpy Roma Downey.

What we know of angels biblically, though, is varied and vague. Gabriel, Raphael, Michael are named. Cherubim are at the east of Eden, Jacob wrestles with one, and an angel goes ahead of the Israelites into the Promised Land. Isaiah sees seraphs at the Lord's throne and is seared by them. Angels appear in psalms and intervene from time to time in the lives of prophets, priests, and the chosen people. Angels sing glorias and signal shepherds to Bethlehem, comfort Jesus after threefold temptation in the desert, minister to him in Gethsemane, guard an empty tomb, spring Peter from prison, figure in apocalyptic battle. Yet what we know of them is precious little.

The name, *aggelos* (angelos) in Greek and *malak* in Hebrew, means, simply, "messenger." In today's readings, the mother of Samson and wife of Manoah and also Zechariah, father of John the Baptizer, husband of Elizabeth, and priest of the order of Abijah, receive messages from angels. Zechariah quibbles and, for several seasons and a pregnancy's length, goes mute. The unnamed mother of Samson asks for no explanation, reports the

63

incident, goes home to await a birth, and presumably keeps talking. After what may have been gauzy apparitions but certainly clear, strong voices speaking in their dialects, Zechariah and Elizabeth, Manoah and wife, watched their small segment of divine destiny unfold.

Angels have achieved a faddish and fascinated interest in the 1990s. None of us, though, can be sure we know what or who they are or whether we have been visited by them. Some suspect as much, others hope so, but none are certain without question.

What we do know, however, is that many messengers of God speak to us each day—in sunrise and Scripture, in purple shadow and sacrament, in friend and in the fathers and mothers of the church, in liturgical splendor and inner voice, in clockwork event and unexpected opportunity, in *cause célèbre* and personal crisis. We require prayer and discernment and sound spiritual direction so that we can tell which hunches, intuitions, nagging doubts, pressing demands call for our standstill, which call for our follow-through. Angels may take myriad forms. They can make eminent sense of our lives and determine our destinies. We need a discipleship of seeing, hearing, faithful knowing, however, if any angelic messengers are to get through. We need a discipleship too that walks us home and yet also moves us on.

For further reflection:

• What, in my life, have I acted on with a kind of blind faith? What were the consequences of my acting?

• When I have a kind of sixth sense that something is to happen and that I may be called to play an active role, how do I test out that sense? Where and to whom do I turn for guidance?

December 20

Isaiah 7:10–14 and Luke 1:26–38

Again the Lord spoke to Ahaz, saying, Ask a sign of the Lord your God;
let it be deep as Sheol or high as heaven.
Isaiah 7:10-11

God's promises are kept—in a ton and tumble of ways. Though, like Ahaz, we may hesitate to ask, dread to tempt, or, like Mary, we may quietly wonder, welcome, and affirm, we have the advantage of the Christian era. We can name the signs and assurances of God's troth and God's truth with extremes of confidence.

We have lived to see this time.

We awaken with Godlight and dawnlight, no matter how darkened or shortened our days.

We have our senses, hearing sounds of morning, feeling the press of flannel against our chill, smelling, then tasting the first draughts of coffee with milk, seeing the streaks of light across new sky. We know, from deep within, that there is a God with whom we may begin to speak and a communion of saints that surrounds us even in our silence. We have been touched with moments of beauty and wisdom, and, even in our tears, we have known a depth of love.

The day begins with a pledge that we ourselves, in the midst of our routines and our unknowings, pack more meaning and hold more promise than we know.

Our names may never be remembered, may not in some sense even matter. In that same sense, neither did Mary's, nor did Ahaz's. But their signs and promises held.

So do ours. So do we.

Emmanuel becomes incarnate again in our smallest things.

For further reflection:

• In a way, we may say with Qoheleth (of Ecclesiastes) that nothing matters, all is vanity. In a way, we may also say with Thérèse of Lisieux that everything does—in its little way. How do I daily experience my non-meaning, non-mattering? When and how do I know that all I am and all I do does have meaning, does matter?

• How, in the course of the days, do I express gratitude to God for his "with-ness" to me?

December 21

Song of Songs 2:8–14 or Zephaniah 3:14–18 and Luke 1:39–45

[F]or now the winter is past, the rain is over and gone. The flowers appear on the earth; and the voice of the turtledove is heard in our land.
Song of Songs 2:11–12

It is one of the ironies of Advent that on the first day of winter in the northern hemisphere this reading from the Song of Songs declares winter's end. December 21 is the shortest, darkest day. Yet it also comes with an assurance that tomorrow, and the days after, will only lengthen again.

What the reading speaks to, of course, is an end to a winter of the spirit. The prophet Zephaniah, in the day's alternative reading, promises that God will warm and awaken us: "He will rejoice over you with gladness, he will renew you in his love" (Zep 3:17). The Song of Songs has been celebrated by the likes of St. Bernard of Clairvaux as a hymn of praise for God's love for the soul and the soul's passion for God. A long tradition holds that it allegorizes an understanding of Christ as bridegroom and the church as bride, seeking one another and consumed in love. In the 1980s French film *Thérèse,* a film done in sepia and yellow and caramel tones, the voice overlay and English subtitles were riddled with lines from this grand canticle. Its lines sweep, gush, long, accelerate, relax, linger, crescendo again, climax, slow, remember. For all its spiritual and ecclesial applications, the Song of Songs is a fully erotic poem. It is rife with sighs, hard breathing, hollowing out, rush, implosion, and a hundred images of fruit, flowers, trees, rivulets, gardens, homes, towns, gems, treasure, daybreak, gold, night. In today's passage the love is gazelle and stag. Figs plump out. Vines spring into fragrant blossom. Three times in seven verses, the woman wonders over "my beloved." Twice the lover invites her, "Arise, my love…" He calls her "fair one" and urges her to "come away" (Sg 2:10, 13).

If the Song of Songs is a key to Christian spirituality, then it seems to reveal the secret of the love we command and preach in our churches. Love requires a heartbeat. Love must be embodied and full of breath. It cannot remain mere abstraction or whim. Love cannot survive as immaterial wish.

Love demands incarnation.

It must stir a human heart, speak with a human voice, invite and respond in human flesh, express itself in human action.

Love calls for festoons of greenery, seed cones, flowers, nuts, fruit. It demands music, brass and drums and strings and reeds, choirs to give it voice. Love needs swish of colored vesture and curtains, incense, candlelight, vessels of gold. And yet love can't be mere pageantry. It can only be love if we give warm, genuine smile and open ourselves to embrace and be embraced.

For love to last we must have faith—faith in our own capacities to be lovers, faith too that there is so much lovable in us. We must be able to trust the life which stirs within us, and we must have confidence in all that we have been lovingly promised.

Mary and Elizabeth in today's gospel held within themselves such faith and trust. They lovingly conceived love, bore love, bodied it forth, and knew that lovework and lifebreath are of God.

For further reflection:

• How today, and in days to come, can I hear the heartbeat under Scripture?

• How can I better come to know and embody God's lovework in me, in family, in city, in church?

December 22

1 Samuel 1:24–28 and Luke 1:46–56

*"For this child I prayed, and the Lord has granted me
the petition that I made to him."*
1 Samuel 1:27

Here are women whose names we know: Hannah and Mary. Here are
women whose canticles live on, indeed, as theme and variation. Hannah's
canticle follows the passage read today, the passage in which she takes young
Samuel, with her offerings, to Shiloh. The child Samuel remains with the
priest Eli, preparing for his own unique call as prophet for Israel (1 Sm 2:11).
Mary's canticle, her Magnificat, as is well-known, parallels Hannah's song of
praise and son-offering. Victory, triumph over disgrace and over God's enemies, the overturn of superficialities and worldly honors, the expectation of
a God-sent child, an unexpected life: all of these are themes of Hannah of
Ramathaim and Mary of Nazareth.

Today we might write our own Christian Magnificat, in a mode something like this:

My heart, my soul, the whole of my life-force rise up
to exult again: I am alive, and I am alive with God's life!
Against all odds, I have seen a deaf and mute man preach,
a blind woman approach the lectern in church to read,
a lost child find himself,
a drunk instruct a class on hope and healing, sobriety and
    sanctity,
gay men and lesbians teach families love and faithfulness,
a circle of broken people embrace one another and, piece by
    piece, grow whole,
and, ill some thirty years, I burst with energy and health.

Winter's ice cracks, and stiffened limbs go supple again.

Purple, white, and yellow flowers fleck wide grasses
where recently was frozen soil and dry rock.
Rivers rise.

God is indeed with us.
In Christ, in the Spirit of Love,
we find fears zeroed out,
our wayward selves brought home,
and all the world's outcast and lovelorn held before us
as lifesign and heartwarm.

I flow to *we*,
and through us flows the Trinity.

We green.
We go on Eastering.

For further reflection:

• Advent to Christmas, Lent to Easter, Pentecost to our every day: How do
these all connect in my faith-life, my loves, my ministry?

December 23

Malachi 3:1–4, 23–24 and Luke 1:57–66

But who can endure the day of his coming, and who can stand when he appears?
For he is like a refiner's fire…
Malachi 3:2

The prophetic figure, the messenger who works "like a refiner's fire" and comes like wildfire himself, figures in religious art, poetic utterance, and apocalyptic imagination from ancient days. Malachi proclaims him, with a wary "Lo!" We don't know what will come of prophets and their warnings, and we don't know what will become of us if we heed them.

Carvings in wood and terra-cotta capture the prophetic spirit, the bombast of Elijah, the gusto of John the Baptizer. In the third floor atrium at the Detroit Institute of Art, two dark torsos entitled "Prophet" grace the north walkway which squares the inner court. Gabriel Joly, a Frenchman who worked in Spain as the Reformation gained momentum, captures the godliness of ancient Israel. One of the figures, bearded, in a headdress that appears like a firm cloth helmet, swirled in a sort of thin stole which snakes around his tunic, seems to be facing, head on, a stiff wind. The prophet, eyes intent and fixed, almost transfixed, will prevail. He clutches a framed board, a tablet, in his left hand. The man who has heard and seen bears an urgent word. He is somehow wild with it, yet also firm and strong.

The older figure, also entitled "Prophet," looks less wind-battered yet steady, accustomed to enduring. The prophetic tablet is in his right hand. Weathered and deliberate, this prophet too will prevail—not because of his own strength but because of the surety of God.

Both figures could be Elijah, in middle years and then older. Or the first could be a mature John the Baptizer, the one into whom the child of today's gospel grew. The second could be Elijah, the one who may still come back, perhaps from a quieted whirlwind. John the Baptizer prepares the way, says Christianity. Elijah prophesies and returns to prophesy again, says

Judaism. Both herald. Both say: Here is our God.

Another figure stands in the second floor, east side, the Detroit River side, in the Italian gallery. The terra-cotta carving attributed to Giovanni D'Antonio Minelli Dei Bardi comes from Padua, from the time just after Columbus' discovery and the incipient map-makings of Vespucci. This John carries a small book, metal-clasped, in his left hand. His lips are parted as if they could call to attention, rage, or break into a smile. His clothing is rangy-looking—vest and loin covering of woven hair, animal skin neither smoothed nor tanned, belted with a rope. He looks like a man who knows energetic activity and fasting, a man of prominent cheekbones. He is not battered by headwind but stands in calm.

All of these speak to the readings of the day. The woodcarved prophets reflect the steadfastness of hope and faith, the perseverance over the centuries in covenant and messianic hope. The message of God, the "Hear, O Israel," echoes throughout the ages because of the intensity and single-heartedness of Elijah and the prophets at large who stood firm, walked forward, weathered abuse and storm, always faced Godward.

The terra-cotta figure is the readied man of Earth, an inheritor of hope who comes forth from desert already refined in the fire. He is the sure man who can stand still in hope's day, in the nowness of Messiah. The gaze is not the somewhat glazed, far-off look of Joly's prophet, emboldened by a future glimmer. His, instead, is the insistent, close-up look at the imminence and immediacy of saving grace, of living Lord.

The carved prophetic figures bear tablets, one in the right hand, one in the left. The terra-cotta Baptist bears his small book in his left hand. The right hand of God comes—Yeshua, Jesus, who needs no book. The prophets and the Baptizer carry testament with them, in heart and in hand. They bespeak and re-speak living word. The one who comes now is living testament, living word, indeed and finally the very last word.

And what has become of us? We are challenged to search our hearts to know in truth how well we bear that word in heart and hand. Have we, no matter how well baptized and catechized, really let ourselves be refined in that fire?

For further reflection:

• How steadfastly do I actually proclaim the nearness and nowness of God amid my crowded life and conflicted city? How clear is my gaze on the one and only thing necessary? Is there any risk that artist or writer or friend would ever perceive in me a passion for God worth memorializing in tome or gallery?

December 24: Mass in the Morning

2 Samuel 7:1–5, 8–11, 16 and Luke 1:67–79

*"By the tender mercy of our God, the dawn from on high will break upon us,
to give light to those who sit in darkness and the shadow of death,
to guide our feet into the way of peace."*
Luke 1:78–79

In our time, daybreak signals the skyward lift of helicopters to survey the major arteries into cities, Monday through Friday. The traffic report, the night-breaking news, the weather forecast are the incantations to which we attend as we shower, gulp our java, dress, and dash from apartment or house into the business of the day.

If we are in the habit of rising early, we may notice the dazzle of sun bulging up, behind and then above the trees, on Saturday and Sunday at least. Or we may vacation for a few days in a calm place where we can watch the sun break over ocean or lake while grass is still dewy or ice on branches and dried reeds still has a diamond glint. Otherwise, we are generally too rushed to let the sunrise spill through thin mist, turn our world to sparkle, and soak us in shine. We miss the splendor of what begins, morning upon morning, and forget how the world warms.

Zechariah, undumbed on the day of the circumcision of his son, noticed beyond the everyday and knew the depth of a new birth. He prophesied the imminent coming of the Savior, the fulfillment of the house of David, the active compassion of God. One would have to be a person who has searched the heart of things, has been attuned to the work of the holy, a person who had often watched dawn's burgeoning light and not quite lost the capacity for wonder to sing his canticle.

As much as a thousand years before Zechariah, David had the impulse to erect a dwelling place for God. Through the prophet Nathan, he heard both God's promise and God's resistance. His kingdom would last, his throne would endure, but he would not be the one to build a temple, he who

74

had been called from pastures and wide sky.

As we, three thousand years after David, prepare to break into our celebration of Christmas, we remember, in new light, David's kingship, his throne, a night star, a breaking light, and the One who comes to reveal that he himself is light, that he himself is where God dwells, that he is, at last, the way to peace.

The Christ who comes as dawnlight, day by day and again and again, steals, up by up, over our horizons, suffuses us with glow, and waits for us to stand still long enough so that we can be drenched in pale yellow fire. He burns away our mist, and he lights the road to where he dwells, which is, if we walk peaceably, everywhere: around us, among us, within us. Wherever we let saving light fall.

He dawns. He dwells. We can be, out of darkness, lighthouse and temple.

For further reflection:

• When have I been especially aware of daybreak, literally? When have I been aware of God's light breaking upon me?

• The late Ann O'Hara Graff, in *In the Embrace of God* (Orbis Books, 1995), has said: "The recognition that we come from God and are going to God, that we belong to God, that we dwell within the embrace of God and are capable of being the dwelling place of God who may dwell in us—these recognitions of our intimacy with our creator are ancient in Christianity" (p. 1). What does it mean to me, as believer and Christ-bearer, to be a "dwelling place of God"? How would I describe the decor of the dwelling I offer for God? How do I illumine this dwelling within?

CHRISTMAS

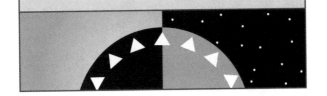

Christmas Vigil

Isaiah 62:1–5 and Matthew 1:1–25 or 1:18–25

You shall be a crown of beauty in the hand of the Lord,
and a royal diadem in the hand of your God.
Isaiah 62:3

Christmas is a sensory fiesta. Liturgically we begin at dark with priests and deacons vested in gold or glinting white, with candlelight and garland and sprays of evergreen, with manger scenes, caroling, handbells, full organ or even orchestra, pungent pine scent, incense, pyramids of poinsettias, the proclamation of a genealogy, the familiar and miraculous bread and wine.

Bells, ornamented trees, santas and snowmen, cascades of lights, candy canes, chimes, "Jingle Bells," old-time sleighs, packages ribboned and bowed, tinsel, glitter, angel-topped trees dazzle city street and shopping mall, rural homestead and village square. Cookies, candies, rum-soaked cakes, hot chocolate, mulled cider, and mistletoed kisses await chapped and wind-licked visitors.

Tastes, smells, sights, sounds, touches render Christmas eve stimulating, heartlifting, magical. Isaiah uses sensuous marital imagery to speak of God's love. He calls us "Delight." Matthew recounts a family line, fourteen generations at a time. It is so obvious that sometimes we overlook how richly Christmas is a celebration of bodily life and family life.

It is good to be born, the Christchild declares. It is good to be an earthling. It is good to have a body which receives and gives sensory delight. It is good to feel the softness of cloth, the padding of straw, a mother's touch. It is good to cry and suck. It is good to open our eyes to watch and follow movement and light. It is good to be astonished at star sparkle. It is good to know the musty smell of barn and animals and to detect the human scents of cooking, firetending, love. It is good to hear soothing voices and song. The Incarnation reminds us that sleep, heartbeat, awakening, holding, being held, eating, drinking, reaching to stroke hair and touch a face, recognizing kin, breathing, sighing, simply being, are and can ever be godly.

Isaiah reminds us of the history of a people. Matthew reminds us of the history of a family. Neither are impeccable. Neither are all sweetness and light. Saints and scoundrels live and die and are our ancestry. Flesh and bone, blood and milk make salvation history, form the God-with-us story, generation after generation.

Christmas, as a star bursts through a darkness, as we wrap ourselves toward midnight, reminds us that we don't "get" God until we get God in our skin.

We are and have spirit. But our spirit is embodied. God's own being, Love, communes with our spirit only through our senses, through our tangible, material being. Thus, we can properly say that revelation is always mediated, always somehow bodily. If it is not, it can't be received. Not by humans beings, anyway.

For further reflection:

In *Retrieving Fundamental Theology* (Paulist Press, 1993), Gerald O'Collins offers this remark:

> Some years ago in England a friend with nerves of steel took one biblical genealogy as his text for the weekend retreat he led. He fed the prayer of his retreatants with the theme of God guiding human history and preparing for the birth of Jesus himself. Given the checkered career of some who are featured in our biblical genealogies, including those of Jesus himself…, one can be helped to a deeper grasp of the truth that "God writes straight but with crooked lines" (p. 133)

• As I review my own family history, where do I detect "crooked lines" with which God, in the end, seems to have written straight? How have grace and good come of some less-than-best family events?

• What bodily delight do I recall fondly tonight as I greet Christmas and gather with family?

Christmas: Mass at Midnight

Isaiah 9:1–6 and Luke 2:1–14

But there will be no gloom for those who were in anguish...
The people who walked in darkness have seen a great light;
those who lived in a land of deep darkness—on them light has shined.
Isaiah 9:1, 2

The twentieth century has been one of tremendous scientific advance, breakthroughs in medical research, marvels of technology which speed communications and travel. The age of information has come upon us, and intimate connections among peoples globally can now be made. Yet the century has also displayed for us the horrors of war and the hazards of irrational hate ratcheted up to untold madness. Pogroms, holocausts, ethnic bloodbaths, terrorist bombings, defoliated jungles and immolated villages, and the ever wracking threat of nuclear weaponry, chemical warfare, wholesale biocide have marked the century. Our wars have left behind napalm and land mines, severed limbs and shattered minds, mass graves and wastelands.

Isaiah, nine centuries before Christ, told of God's dream for us: a time when warriors' boots and bloodied garments would be burned (Is 9:5). In messianic time, in a time of childgift, the reign of peace would be ushered in.

The same dream of peace on Earth is sung in the praise of the heavenly hosts over Bethlehem, at night, over flocks and shepherds' watch. God's dream for us at the turn of our common era two thousand years ago remained the same as God's dream for us in the time of proto-Isaiah. The dream has yet to come true.

The first Mass of Christmas comes into the somberness of night. It is marked by nocturnal beauty: faint scents of pine, flickering candle, the glints of golden chalices and brocade vestments. But if we stand outside, away from illuminated windows and streetlights, we know that all we have is moon and starlight. If we are northerners, snow may lighten our landscape and give us a line of sight. But cloud and shadow remain, and we might as well be walking through a tunnel of smoke.

In the grip of gloom, in the constraint of night, we must somehow supply our own light. But if we are to see in more than a small circle or farther than the stream of headlight or searchlight, we need lights which others supply too. We find our way from darkness only with Godlight, otherlight, our light all streaming—and streaming together.

The long persistence of war and the stranglehold of hate are possible because we continue to hoard light, douse light, or close ourselves in darkness. The coming to be of peace is possible only if, individually and collectively, we allow ourselves to be gentled by darkness and to acknowledge our mutual need. We must let ourselves be softened by starlight, by sheep lowing, by the snorings of laborers, by the cries of a newborn. In the midst of night's silence, we must allow ourselves to listen for the harmony of spheres and "praisesong." To change our minds to peace, we must train our hearts to trust and welcome.

A background of Hallelujah choruses may help. But one by one we must decide to ignite our light and unclench our fists.

For further reflection:

• Traversing the space from hope to realization can sometimes seem like a dreadful task. When have I seen peacemaking, or some reconciliation, work? What had to change in persons, in me, for it to happen?

Christmas: Mass at Dawn

Isaiah 62:11–12 and Luke 2:15–20

The shepherds returned, glorifying and praising God for all they had heard and seen, as it had been told them.
Luke 2:20

Probably the best news that we can receive is that we are specially loved and specially favored by someone who inspires love in us, calls forth the best from us, and assures us that we have the possibility and power of reshaping our lives.

People dream of such possibility daily and give the dreams material expression by entering sweepstakes, purchasing lottery tickets, speculating on the stock market, investing in a long shot, hiring financial planners and personal trainers, joining health clubs, starting therapy, cultivating the company of celebrities, feeding fantasies, smoking pipe dreams, falling cyclically into infatuations. We hope for jackpots and keep coming up with small change.

The shepherds' story—their hillside astonishment, their pursuit of mother, carpenter, and manger, the news and memory which they carried back—makes all other winnings, success stories, bestowals of good fortune, gala cruises, romantic adventures, strokes of genius, felicitous moments, and dreams-come-true pale by comparison. The epiphany of the Christ-coming which the shepherds were able to gaze upon and partake of must, we swear, have quelled desire, quieted restiveness, settled old grudges, eased burdens, sweetened bitterness, stilled envy and lightened their hearts. The shepherds at Bethlehem that night touched transcendence. They heard, saw, and God's favor penetrated, permeated. *Cor ad cor loquitur.* Out of nowhere came this heart-to-heart, this voice of blessing and benefaction.

Isaiah says that when salvation is proclaimed it names people. It calls them "Holy," "Redeemed," "Sought Out," "a City Not Forsaken" (Is 62:12), children of light, a populace of grace.

So precisely were the shepherds called.

So, as Christ is reborn in us—as he must be in every generation and indeed in every heart—are we called.

We can be new, sought out and found, found and embraced.

Christ's coming and coming and coming again can move us to praise, can wake us to glory. But only if we recall that he has come to us, for us, out of sheer favor.

For further reflection:

In 1984, the Black Catholic Bishops of the United States issued a pastoral letter on evangelization, "What We Have Seen and Heard." The title was drawn from 1 Jn 1:1–4. That text, which emphasizes how impelled believers are to proclaim what they have experienced in the person of Christ, echoes the story of the shepherds in today's gospel. They hear, see, and must go out and tell. The Black Bishops say, in the opening of that letter, that "the mature Christian community feels the irresistible urge to speak that Word."

• How does my Christian community show that it finds that urge "irresistible"? How am I impelled personally by the gospel?

Christmas: Mass During the Day

Isaiah 52:7–10 and John 1:1–18 or 1:1–5, 9–14

...[A]nd all the ends of the earth shall see the salvation of our God.
Isaiah 52:10

For all the televangelists' rant about being saved and its necessity, for all the street corner accosters' urgency about our being born-again before Armageddon, the rapture, or whatever, we may find ourselves wondering what salvation truly means. What does it do? How does it change things?

The fleetfoot messenger hailed in Isaiah offers us the first fact about salvation: "Your God reigns" (Is 52:7). From the beginning of his public life and at the heart of his parables and miracles is that same proclamation made by Jesus: the arrival of God's kingdom, the assertion of God's rule. It is not as if God somehow, for a stretch of centuries, gave up sovereignty over the world of life. But it does seem that humans needed, and have continued to need, a saving figure, a Christus who can speak the truth with such clarity and enact it with such integrity that we have to assent, yes, that God does reign. Yes, God's goodness overcomes. The vise of fear and death and hate and destructiveness loosens, and, in the end, divine and human love go free. The triumph of God's reign is the only sure win.

A second explanation of what salvation means comes from the opening of John's gospel. The Word who embodies the reign of God reveals that God's being, God's performative word upon us, is "life, and the life [is] the light of all people" (Jn 1:4). Salvation is, then, life and radiance—in their fullness.

A third point about salvation is how it sets right and makes clear our relationships. We are "children of God," sons and daughters, insofar as we have "received" the Word, "believed in his name," claimed the power given us as pure grace (Jn 1:12). Salvation is universal in its offer, mystical in its bonding.

A fourth point is that salvation means, incessantly "grace upon grace"

(Jn 1:16). As far as God is concerned, we cannot be surfeited with gifts. Every one that comes to us is precious, and every one is necessary.

Where the *New Revised Standard Version* reads the Word, the son, as "grace and truth" streamed upon us, the *New American Bible* translates that incarnate "grace and truth" as "enduring love" (Jn 1:14 and 17). We may say, then, from *"pleres charitos kai aletheias"* and *"e charis kai e aletheia"* in the Greek, that we have been made for gift upon gift, truth upon truth. We have been made for lasting love.

Our carols and illumined trees, our elegantly wrapped packages and carefully selected greetings, our pilgrimages to homesteads and our full-house churchgoings are sign and reminder: that God is over all; that we are meant to live fully and live in light; that grace awaits us to the extent that we are receptive; that relatedness and truth widen our hearts and outstretch our arms.

The Lord is come.

In other words, there is no need to stand for isolation, darkness, dread, no need to succumb to forces that fray and frighten and falsify.

We need to sing again so we will know.

Salvation.

It falls upon us as easily as a soft, moonlit night of snow.

For further reflection:

• What about Christmas particularly reminds me that our God reigns?

• Who, during the past year, has uniquely taken the role of Isaiah's beautiful, swift-footed messenger to remind me of God's "enduring love"?

• How can I give the gift of Christmas during the coming year?

Afterword

Around the globe, we find God with us in the shimmer of lakes, in great icicles hanging from cliffs, in burgeoning trees, in the v-formations of Canadian geese, in sunsets and expanses of sand, in the bleat of sheep and in wolf howl, in the men and women and children we shelter and serve, in symphony and song, in dance and drama and artwork, in adventure and science, in people we can hold and kiss, in word and sacraments and saints. Emmanuel attunes us to the manifold ways in which we can meet God. God pours on us like afternoon light from cloudbreak and squooshes under our feet on muddy pathways. God crackles around us like fallen twigs and thumps against us like woodpecker breaking through bark. God signals us from our communications satellites and lights up our computer screens. Our rumpled God asks us for a handout from a stake-out on a steam grate around a city corner, and our tender God calls us aside to wonder how we are. God lingers over our first cup of morning coffee and wafts around our daydreams. The Incarnation has more meanings than we can ever hope to name.

One, of course, is the scandal of anti-transcendence: the shock of a God who knows sweat, sorrow, desire, joy, fatigue, comfort, ache, gratitude, loneliness, intimacy, distance, closeness, birth, infancy, childhood, adolescence, maturity and death—by having lived them. The Incarnation means that God knows exactly what it is to wake and breathe in human skin, to feel with human sense and nerve, to think human thoughts. God has had the experience of our confusion and our clarity. God has made the anti-infinity, anti-eternity move of being in Earth time and living with Earth limits.

Another meaning of the Incarnation is that the "withness" of God has cosmic consequences. With the incarnate coming of Christ and with resurrection faith in his enduring presence, we gather that God has not only flung galaxies out and away from Godself in pinwheels of matter and light but also made bone, flesh, blood for himself out of our planetary elements, compounds, nutrients. God has drenched Godself in starstuff and Earthdust. If we believe this, there can never be "mere" matter.

The Incarnation means too that God has glorified and magnified the simplest human touches. We have inscribed paintings on cave walls, cuneiform on tablets, symbols in rocks, words on pages simply to express ourselves, simply to let someone know what we have thought or loved. Jesus of Nazareth has left stories, favorite sayings, pronouncements, parables, and we, to this day, explicate and apply the gospels and uncover meaning upon meaning. Over the centuries we have made galas and Taj Mahals, yet we have also crafted small memorials and commonplace tokens of love: rocks piled a certain way, grain laid in tombs, candles lit, toasts made, blessings prayed. God in Christ has left us with washings in water and bread and wine shared. In doing so, he has left not only memorial but also a partaking in his aliveness. Two thousand years later, we still barely begin to realize the magnitude of such simple gifts.

God's being in the world as Messiah, as Emmanuel, also means that "I love you" never means only two, face to face, locked in embrace, rocking to sleep. "I love you" means that God swirls about and spirals cyclonic yet gentle through that love. "I love you," in Emmanuel, wants always to widen out. The Incarnation means that we can be lovemakers in a world of ruffians and shepherds, a world of timid souls and magi, a world of folks who beckon us and those who put us off, a world of friends and strangers. The Incarnation promises us that there is warmth and light enough.

That, in sum, though not in conclusion, is what Christmas opens, a world of hope.

In Joyful Expectation
Advent Prayers and Reflections
Laurin Wenig

The daily prayers and reflections found in this book use the Scripture readings for Advent for all three cycles. The author's experience of living in Israel is shared in the reflections and prayers. The questions focus on bringing together the reader's lived experiences and the longing for the Savior.

120 pp, $7.95 (order M-01)

Preparing for Christmas
J.D. Crichton

The author gives detailed pastoral commentaries on the readings for the last seven days of Advent, and points out the significance of the great "O" antiphons which are sung on these days. Enriches the celebration of the Advent liturgies.

82 pages, $6.95 (order L-63)

With Hearts on Fire
Reflections on the Weekday Readings of the Liturgical Year
Rev. Joseph Donders

At last—a book that offers homilists a reflection on each of the weekday gospel readings! These reflections aim to help both homilist and assembly accompany Jesus and his first disciples in their ministry, as described by the evangelists. Fr. Donders' sound insights and practical applications—which emphasize Jesus' message of justice and love—will enrich your relationship to the daily gospel readings. The answer to a homilist's prayer!

352 pp, $19.95 (order J-22)

Advent and Lent Activities for Children
Camels, Carols, Crosses, and Crowns
Shiela Kielly and Sheila Geraghty

Bells, birds, and Boxing Day...manger, magi, and mistletoe...In this fascinating collection, the authors explore many of the customs and traditions surrounding the seasons of Advent and Lent (Christmas and Easter, too). It is a lively and interesting read, filled with ideas that will be of great value to parents, teachers, catechists, pastors, and lay ministers.

128 pp, $9.95 (order M-51)

Available at religious bookstores or from:

TWENTY-THIRD PUBLICATIONS
P.O. BOX 180 • 185 WILLOW ST. • MYSTIC, CT 06355 • 1-860-536-2611 • 1-800-321-0411 • FAX 1-860-572-0788

Call for a free catalog